PLANNING AND PREPARATION

UNIVERSITY INTERVIEWS
Top answers & insider tips

IAN STANNARD AND GODFRE

trotman | t

University Interviews: Top answers & insider tips

This first edition published in 2017 by Trotman Education, an imprint of Crimson Publishing Ltd, 19–21c Charles Street, Bath, BA1 1HX

© Crimson Publishing Ltd, 2017

Authors: Ian Stannard and Godfrey Cooper

British Library Cataloguing in Publication Data
A catalogue record for this book is available from the British Library

ISBN: 978 1 911067 55 9

Typeset by IDSUK (DataConnection) Ltd
Printed and bound in Malta by Gutenberg Press Ltd

CONTENTS

PREFACE

"We find ourselves in a dilemma. We have an increasing number of applicants and most have very similar academic profiles. This means that it is harder than ever to pick the right people for the places. We use the interview as a key discriminator. It is therefore my strong advice that you take the time to prepare for this event properly. Spend at least as much time as you spent on the personal statement."

ADMISSIONS TUTOR, IMPERIAL COLLEGE, LONDON

Who is this book aimed at?

Well, the simple answer is anyone who is leaving school and likely to be interviewed for a job, university place or higher apprenticeship. The bias in the book is heavily weighted towards the university sector. However, interviews are part of professional life and the skills that you need to thrive are important and transferable.

Schools in the UK are very good at preparing pupils for exams. They know how to help them revise and provide them with opportunities to practise their skills in mocks. However, many very good schools do not teach the 'soft skills' that people need. These include the art of giving presentations, leadership, etiquette in different social situations, how to write a report or formal letter, how to manage your finances and, most relevant to this book, how to prepare for and do well in an interview. This is vital not only for an application to university but also for life beyond school. Top employers complain about the lack of these skills in both school and undergraduate applicants.

This book will provide you with the guidance you need to produce a first-class performance at interview. The preparation of your personal statement for university entrance or your curriculum vitae (CV) for a higher or degree apprenticeship gets you to the starting gate, but it is your performance at interview that secures the place.

This book will cover the planning and preparation you need to do prior to attending an interview, the psychology of the interview process, the interview itself and the types of interview you may face.

In the book, tips for success and tips to avoid failure at interview are also given. There is a presumption that you intend to apply to university, so if you need help in the process of choosing a course and writing a personal statement too, then I would point you to the book *How to Write a Winning UCAS Personal Statement*, published by Trotman Education. This was written by Ian Stannard, has been well received and is in its third edition.

The principles of success are always the same. If you prepare properly you will succeed, but if you fail to prepare – be prepared to fail. Interviews are competitive and any edge you bring to the process will help. Take on board the advice given and make sure that you do not omit any part of the guidance given in this book.

INTRODUCTION

"The interview is a key part of the application process and it is vital that the candidate prepares carefully. It is not about tricking you or making you look foolish. When we interview, one of the key questions we ask ourselves is 'Do we want this person in our department?'"
UNIVERSITY OF LONDON

"Interviews can range from an 'exam out loud' to an informal chat designed to encourage you to choose that course. Some are competitive and others just marketing orientated. Most are the latter so don't panic but do some research so you are not caught out. They can last anything from ten minutes to an hour and are usually, though not always, conducted by one interviewer. Most are one to one, but some can be group too! Again – do some research – ask questions in advance."
FORMER ADMISSIONS TUTOR, NOW CAREERS TEACHER

"We welcome contact with applicants before they arrive. Never worry about asking questions about what to expect, what to wear or what to do. We are not scary!"
UNIVERSITY OF LONDON

The application

Before you are invited to attend an interview, you must 'sell' yourself on paper. As far as universities are concerned your opportunity to do so comes by way of the preparation and submission of your personal statement. It is not the role of this book to help you prepare a personal statement but it is vital that it is attractive to the admissions team that will read it. By this I mean that the statement is free from spelling and grammatical errors and that colloquial phrases or jokes are avoided.

Furthermore, the statement must sell you in a way that is compelling, engaging and well informed. Your reasons for applying must be strong and this must be evidenced by what you have done to support your application. The competition for some courses is fierce and the admissions officers are looking for ways to reduce the pool of prospective candidates.

"Your personal statement provides very valuable background information, which assists the College in our selection process. Many selectors wish to choose applicants who, as well as being intellectually able to cope with the course of study, will contribute to the creation of an intake with a wide cross-section of interests in each year. Please note that your personal statement should accurately reflect your interests and these may be discussed with you at interview."
IMPERIAL COLLEGE LONDON

Will I be interviewed?

On the positive side, *most universities do not interview candidates*, but you are likely to be interviewed if you apply to the following institutions or courses.

- All Oxbridge candidates – by this I mean Oxford and Cambridge.
- Everyone applying to read medicine, dentistry and veterinary medicine, and all applicants for nursing, midwifery and physiotherapy or other healthcare professions.
- University College London interviews students for popular subjects. One course that calls most people for interview is European Social and Political Studies. Look carefully at the website for up-to-date information.
- King's College London will interview some applicants, particularly law applicants. Look at the website for up-to-date information.
- The University of Warwick interviews most maths applicants.
- Imperial College London interviews most students. These interviews are competitive and play an important part in deciding whether a place is offered. Good advice is available online to help you prepare.

- Lancaster University interviews philosophy applicants to assess them for a bursary award. Check the website for more details and for other courses that offer bursaries.
- All courses leading to qualified teacher status (QTS) are required to carry out a 'screening' interview.
- Art Foundation courses conduct an interview, either face to face or, increasingly, online via Skype. This will be a discussion about your portfolio of work and interests in art or design/architecture.
- Drama colleges often ask for an audition and will interview you at the same time.
- Music students may be interviewed and will certainly have to audition if their course is performance based.

Your online profile

Take a moment to look at your online profile and your social network status. Many employers and universities run a check on your online social network profile. They will be concerned if it includes material that is radically political, sexist, racist or 'offensive'. What you think is inoffensive may seem very different to a middle-aged admissions tutor or employer. If it is not something you want employers or admissions tutors to see, delete it and update your profile! Check and amend privacy filters and start to operate a more mature approach to these things. This is especially true of Facebook or similar sites.

....

"Although it is not likely that every candidate's social media profile will be looked at, I think it is wise to check your online presence and certainly make sure that your privacy settings are valid. This is particularly true if you are applying for a place that may involve a placement with children, in a legal setting, with vulnerable adults or in a medical environment. What I know for sure is that future employers DO care about these things. If in doubt, take action!"

CURRENT STUDENT, THIRD YEAR UNIVERSITY COLLEGE LONDON

Submitted work

Oxbridge colleges ask for marked written work to be submitted in advance of the interview for certain subjects. This is normally an essay or assignment you have completed during your sixth form and one that has been marked by your teacher. Prepare thoroughly and check what work is likely to be needed.

Before the interview, make sure that you re-read the work you submitted and ask yourself some questions. Did I enjoy completing that task? What would I do now to change some of the assumptions I made? If I was in the interviewer's shoes, what questions would I ask about the conclusions I drew or the evidence I presented to support my conclusion?

Admissions tests

Many universities require students to take admissions tests. You need to look carefully at university websites to ascertain what test you might need to take. Most Oxbridge candidates, most medical and dental applicants, some law applicants and many applicants to Imperial College London will be asked to take tests. Warwick asks maths applicants to take a maths test. There are practice papers online and a myriad of guides in print to help you prepare.

However, the onus is on you to find out and, in most cases, arrange to take the tests in a location near your home or at school.

"It is very important to make arrangements in good time, as your application may not be as competitive – or may not be considered at all – if you do not take any test or tests required for your course."
ADMISSIONS, UNIVERSITY OF OXFORD

Subject-specific tests

Some applicants may be asked to take a test before the interview, as part of the selection process, or during the interview, if shortlisted. For instance, students applying to read law may need to take the Law National Aptitude Test (LNAT) and those wanting to read medicine may need to take the BioMedical Admissions Test (BMAT) or the UK Clinical Aptitude Test (UKCAT). Oxford and Cambridge offer a wide range of subject tests, taken in the November or December after you apply. Imperial College London is following suit and may be joined by other top universities.

These types of tests are increasing. Most are subject related. Others are thinking-skills tests that are designed to test your potential or skills. Check carefully what tests, if any, you will need to take by looking at online prospectuses.

Interviews with psychometric and other tests

Students applying for entrance to university rarely undertake psychometric testing. This is more likely to affect applicants for higher apprenticeship schemes.

Numerical reasoning, verbal reasoning and spatial awareness tests

These tests are usually a combination of numerical reasoning, verbal reasoning and spatial awareness. To some extent it is possible to practise for these tests because there are many books on the market. Online practice papers may be available too. Practising will get you used to the style of questions and so save you time during the test. It is not possible to practise specific questions, but those used in the numerical reasoning and verbal reasoning sections all tend to follow similar types of approach.

The numerical reasoning test will require you to do some simple mental calculations and to recognise sequences or patterns in the numbers given. You will be asked to work out the next number in a series or pattern. Some questions will be in the form of graphs.

The verbal reasoning test assesses how your brain processes language, by asking you to recognise synonyms, antonyms and analogies, as well as testing your spelling and grammar. The analogies will often give you a sequence of A is to B followed by C is to ..., with a series of options to choose from.

Regarding spatial awareness, the varieties of questions are enormous, but in general you will be faced with different shapes and patterns and you should identify commonalities and differences. You have to visualise and manipulate three-dimensional shapes. You will be given a choice of answers, and from the shapes given in the question you have to work out which one fits the sequence.

Sometimes the above types of tests are considered to be IQ tests since they cover the full range of mental tests. The tests in most common use are the AH (Alice Heim) series, NIIP (National Institute of Industrial Psychology) tests and Raven's Matrices.

The VA series of tests will help with the verbal reasoning test. The NA series of tests, NC2 or the GMA numerical test will help you to prepare for the numerical reasoning test. The ST series of tests are often used with spatial awareness testing.

All of the above tests are subject to specific time limits, so if there is a question that you cannot readily see the answer to, move on to the next one. For more information, visit the tests' individual websites.

Personality tests

Personality tests and psychological testing are used most often by employers to help with the overall assessment of a candidate. They may therefore form part of the interview process for a degree apprenticeship or higher apprenticeship (see pages 23–24 and Part Three).

The questions in these tests are multiple choice questions that require you to select the option that best describes your personality. These tests are professionally designed by external bodies and the outcome of the candidate's responses will provide a personality profile.

Areas of personality such as Assertiveness, Adaptability, Extrovert/Introvert, Team/Individual preferences, Decisiveness and others are covered in the personality profile. Usually some 16 aspects of personality are included.

There are no right or wrong responses to a given situation. The answers given by a candidate will help the person doing the assessing to see whether the candidate's profile matches the type of role for which they are applying. It is important for candidates to answer the questions truthfully, otherwise they may end up in an apprenticeship/job that is unsuitable or not to their liking.

Because personality tests are a measure of the candidate's personal preferences and interests, it is not possible to prepare for them. The tests usually have a time constraint and part of the reason for this is so that the candidate does not spend too much time trying to analyse what each question means. Candidates should know their own personality and so should try to answer with confidence.

Note: Some employers, such as the armed forces, offer sponsorships to study at university, and personality testing will form part of their selection process.

CHAPTER ONE
THE PSYCHOLOGY OF THE INTERVIEW PROCESS

It is helpful to have some insight into how the interviewer is likely to approach the interview, since it will help you to prepare. In the case of the Oxbridge interview, the candidate will usually have been asked to send some written work in advance. This work may be used as part of the interview process. Other than that, and for most other university interviews, the interviewer has only the personal statement in front of them. The candidate thus has an advantage at the start of the interview. It is critical, therefore, to prepare well by having examples to substantiate the things you have written in your personal statement. It is also vital not to lie in the application, as this will quickly be exposed. If you say that you have read a book, make sure that you have done so!

There are two theories of behaviour that enable an interviewer to learn about the interviewee. Many practitioners favour the theory that in order to predict someone's future behaviour it is important to find out about their past behaviour. This theory is usually called the 'Inertia' model because it is assumed that people's behaviour doesn't change radically over time and that if it does change, then the change is a gradual one. From the age of 18 years onwards the change is likely to be marginal. The Inertia model is important at this stage because work patterns and exam success up to the point of the interview are likely to be mirrored in future performance. There is good evidence to suggest that GCSE performance is a sound indicator of degree classification.

The second theory is called the 'Amoeba' model because it suggests that an individual grows and develops a specific 'behaviour type' as they age. However, to predict how the individual will behave in the future, it is necessary to get to know them very well. Clearly, the university interview is not the place for such a conversation. Therefore, the expectation is that interviewers will favour the first model – past performance as a predictor of future performance. This is why GCSE grades and the school's prediction of A level grades are so important, particularly now that the AS exam is being phased out and all exams are becoming linear. It is also why some universities now use pre-interview testing, such as the BMAT or LNAT, their own bespoke tests, and even 'on the day' assessments to help guide their decision-making process.

Critical incidents or episodes

The interviewer may focus on critical incidents or episodes in the applicant's life because the reply will be based upon the applicant's long-term memory of events. Because we store events in our lives in our long-term memory, they are easily recalled. The interviewer will use these to form a judgement about the applicant.

Each episode has the following properties:

- time – year, month, day, hour
- place
- people involved
- sequence of events
- behaviour.

Many interviewers tend to ask dichotomous questions that give rise to bland 'Yes' or 'No' answers. For example, 'Did you like "x"?' is dichotomous in that it begs the answer 'Yes' or 'No'. Interviewers may ask dichotomous questions because we are brought up to develop this style of questioning on social occasions and do not wish to offend people who we do not know. They are not that useful because they are not demanding and do not highlight or expose a weakness or a strength. Far more insightful are episodic questions, which often include the word 'why' or 'what'. Episodic memory is the collection of past personal experiences that occurred at a particular time and place: the memory of autobiographical events (times, places, associated emotions and other contextual who, what, when, where, why knowledge) that can be explicitly stated or conjured.

Telling the truth

It can be difficult for an interviewer to know whether the interviewee is telling the truth. The psychologists Lindsay and Norman claim that there is a process in the brain whose job is to 'monitor' answers to questions and put the person in a good light, whether the answers are true or not.

In answers to dichotomous questions, if the eyes of the interviewee flick down briefly, then the answer is likely to be untrue. To ensure against the possibility of receiving fabricated answers, the interviewer must ask episodic questions. Answers to these require the brain to picture the event, and while doing so the interviewee will look up. Using episodic questions will avoid untruthful answers. Interviewees are advised always to be truthful because if they are found out the interview will be terminated or an offer of a place will be withdrawn.

"I remember one undergraduate stating that he was the President of the Chemistry Society on his curriculum vitae, but when asked what he actually did, it transpired that he was just a figurehead. I was looking for an episode to demonstrate leadership qualities."

GRADUATE RECRUITMENT EMPLOYER

Here are some examples of dichotomous and episodic questions that are possible in a university or apprenticeship interview. They are all general, not subject specific.

Dichotomous	Episodic
Did you enjoy rugby at school?	What was your worst moment playing rugby while at school?
Did you find schoolwork easy?	What challenges did you face when studying for your A levels?
Did you like being a prefect?	Tell me about the most difficult pupil you had to deal with at school as a prefect.
Did you like being a leader?	Tell me about a time when you led a team of people and had to achieve something collectively.
Do you read widely?	Think about the books you have read recently which helped to develop your knowledge of your chosen subject. Pick one that was particularly influential and explain why.
Why did you choose Oxford?	What concerns do you have about being a student at Oxford?

Cognitive behavioural therapy (CBT)

A recent psychological trend in interview training is to consider the impact of CBT. This is a treatment commonly used in the NHS for a range of psychological challenges, including anxiety, lack of self-confidence and phobias. You can use some of the techniques of CBT to help you prepare for the interview, without having to meet a trained psychologist.

At this point, it is worth considering your mindset. A mindset is a state of mind that influences your attitudes and behaviour. If you have a fixed mindset you are likely to resist and fear change. You will be less likely to take risks, in order to avoid failure. Those with an open mindset are more receptive to new experiences, embrace change and have an optimistic outlook. I mention this as it is important to consider what sort of person you are and whether you have any unhelpful thinking styles that may trap you in an interview.

The fear of failure

You want to get a place and you tell yourself that you cannot fail, otherwise your life will be over!

This plain nonsense is likely to raise your anxiety levels and increase the pressure on you when you arrive for the interview. If you are one of these types, you need to talk yourself out of this thinking. If you do not get a place, your life will not be over. You can apply again, accept another offer or just move to a different path in life and return to this again in the future. The interview is a learning experience and it may well be that you must fail one interview in order to succeed in the next. It is a sobering thought that a good number of medical school applicants who win a place succeed in their SECOND application cycle. The first was a dress rehearsal!

Nerves are not bad

You will feel nervous. Anxiety can focus the mind and make you think clearly. Many successful people need the fear of deadlines to make them get on with their work. I know – I am one of them! When preparing for the interview, accept that nerves are normal and do not think that you will not be able to cope with this pressure.

Sleep is important

It is crucial not to underestimate the importance of sleep when preparing for an exam or interview. The majority of teenagers need between nine and ten hours of sleep a night in order to function normally, but most get less than seven hours, for a whole variety of reasons. 'Adolescents are often sleep-deprived, which may in turn increase vulnerability to stress,' says child psychologist Andrew Fuller. **In the week leading up to the interview** it is important to follow these five rules (simple but hard to follow) that will help you catch up on sleep and arrive at the interview in a good mental state.

- Try to get up at about the same time each morning.
- Do some exercise and go for a walk at least once every day.
- If you're worrying about things during the night, set aside some time for problem-solving during the day.
- Avoid drinks that contain caffeine after 4pm.
- Allow yourself time to wind down before going to bed. If you're working or studying, stop at least 45 minutes before bedtime. **Put your phone, iPad or laptop downstairs!**

ABC

The ABC model is a simple diagnostic tool used in CBT. It will help you to identify any thinking errors you might make before or during the interview. **You may wish to try this as a paper and pen exercise at first, but with practice you will become adept at carrying out ABC formulations mentally.**

A = Adversity (the challenge – your personal goal). Make a note of the aspects of the interview that worry you most. It might be that you will not know the answer, dry up, be late or say something stupid. Once you have made the list, tackle each point on the list one by one, with the help of a parent, teacher or friend. In doing so, you will address these problems openly.

B = Beliefs (thoughts or beliefs about the situation). Use the list of unhelpful thinking styles above as a reference and define any other negative thoughts you may have. Try to be as objective as possible, challenging these thoughts on the basis of their evidence, realism and usefulness. Once you have done this, develop a more constructive thinking strategy that will boost your confidence at interview.

C = Consequences (how you feel and act). Notice the way you feel when engaging in unhelpful thinking (increased anxiety). Do these thoughts and feelings undermine your preparation for the interview (through lack of focus)?

CHAPTER TWO
PLANNING AND PREPARATION

The planning and preparation for the interviews for university or for apprenticeships are covered separately here, although there is some overlap.

Planning and preparation for selecting the university and subject

You need to consider all the following bullet points before writing your personal statement and submitting your application. Should you be invited to an interview, you can expect to have to talk about many of these points.

- Before writing your personal statement, research and decide what subject to study. Think carefully about the content of the course, the areas covered, the specialism of the department and the assessment criteria.
- It is no good applying to a university because it has a good reputation generally. Consider the employment prospects of graduates. What do employers think about the course and the reputation of the university?
- You may have personal reasons for deciding the location of your chosen university, such as finances or proximity to family or friends.
- What accommodation is available at the university? What accommodation is available near to the university? What is the cost of accommodation? How many years is it possible to live in a hall of residence?
- What type of university is it? Is it a campus?
- What financial assistance is there by way of bursaries or hardship funds?
- What sports facilities are available?
- Visit the university to assess for yourself.

Planning and preparation for selecting an apprenticeship

Search online to find out what companies offer apprenticeships in fields that use your knowledge of subjects that you are good at.

- It is important to find out as much as possible about the company you are proposing to apply to. This will help you to decide if it is the sort of company you would like to work for. Visit the company's website. Look at the annual report. Are there any current issues that will affect the company? What is its main business? Obtain its prospectuses and, if possible, phone the company and see whether it is possible to speak to a member of staff who is currently on an apprenticeship.
- Find out about arrangements for day release, what qualifications it will lead to, the timetable of the courses and the subjects that will be covered.
- What is the salary range during the apprenticeship?
- Where are the locations of the factories/labs or offices?
- In case of need, are travel expenses refundable? If an overnight stay is necessary, will the cost be reimbursed?
- If it's necessary to live away from home, are lodging allowances available?
- What would the typical career progression be after qualification?

It is essential to make these enquiries before writing your cover letter because many of these details may need to be covered. Moreover, questions at the interview may well involve some of the points above. See Part Three for further information about degree apprenticeships and some pointers to good websites.

The interview letter arrives!

Hopefully, within a few weeks of sending off your application, you will get a letter inviting you to interview. Do not worry if this takes some time, as some universities wait until the end of the application cycle, normally January, before deciding who to invite. This is not true of Oxbridge, which invites people to interviews in November or December.

The structure of the interview will vary – sometimes it will be one to one, sometimes a panel interview. Sometimes you will be asked to do a group task or to complete a task on the day that you may be asked to comment on. Sometimes the interview is formal and at other times remarkably informal. Medical interviews are often multi-staged, with a variety of mini interviews rather than one long one. Part Two of this book looks at this in more detail and explains the different formats of interviews and what you might expect for different subjects. For instance, applicants for medicine will have a very different style of interview from the type of interview used for engineering applicants at Oxbridge.

Do some homework and read the website carefully. Try to find out the names of the admissions tutors in the department. Sometimes they will give you an idea of the sorts of questions you will be asked and the tasks to be undertaken. Look at social network sites for 'inside tips', BUT be aware that these are not always reliable!

TIME TO BRAINSTORM: INTERVIEW HOMEWORK

At this point I recommend that you pause, find a notepad and a pen and do some brainstorming. Look at the questions below and make some notes.

1 Think again about your motivation to study this subject at university. Make some notes about why you want to study it and why you have chosen to study at this university. Does it offer the best course? Why? Take some time to think about this and brainstorm with family or friends to help.

2 What have you read recently in support of your application? If this is not appropriate, think about things that you could do to further your love or understanding of this subject. Again – take notes.

3 Re-read your personal statement and make sure that you can support any claims you have made in it. Have you read the books you cite recently? Have you read others that you might want to mention too? What did you learn from this extra reading? Practise talking about this with a friend, family member or teacher.

4 Think about any pieces of coursework that you have completed that may be relevant or that you want to bring up at interview. What did you do? What did you learn? How did the process help you to develop useful skills?

5 If you have undertaken work experience before the interview, think carefully and note the following. What you did Why it is relevant. For how long, and what you learnt. If you did anything specific or your own or under supervision, be ready to explain this at interview.

6 What independent learning have you done recently? What initiatives have you taken? What leadership skills can you talk about? Take notes of the answers to these questions.

7 Start to prepare answers to some of the common questions you will be asked (see Part Two) and then PRACTISE answering them.

8 Arrange a mock interview – ideally with someone who you do not know that well. Many schools will offer this if you ask for it.

9 Think about the final questions part of an interview. What would you ask? Don't ask banal, dull questions such as 'What is the accommodation like?' Ask instead about postgraduate opportunities, employment statistics for recent graduates, the range of teaching methods employed or assessment criteria – is it all exams or is there coursework assessment too? These are better questions and they show your ambition.

CHAPTER THREE

INTERVIEW FORMATS

Interviews tend to follow one of three principal formats – **the panel or one-to-one interview**, **the group interview and the multiple mini interview (MMI)**.

The panel or one-to-one interview

This format is very common in degree apprenticeship interviews and for non-medical university applications. Here the candidate will sit with an interviewer or, in the case of a panel, with two or more interviewers, and a conversation will follow. This is the common format for Oxbridge interviews and can be the most daunting as you are on your own.

The group interview

This format is common in medical interviews and can be used alongside the one-to-one interview. Group interviews are more informal and often they are used to assess your communication and listening skills, leadership and initiative. Drama schools often use **group workshops** to see how people interact with others.

The MMI

This format is fairly new and now common in selection for medicine, dentistry, veterinary medicine, social work and professions allied to medicine. There is more information in Part Two, but in essence MMIs are best explained with a quote from Brighton and Sussex Medical School (BSMS), who describes them thus: '*The Multiple Mini Interviews (MMI) at BSMS will consist of five discussions, each lasting ten minutes, with a minute between each discussion. Applicants will move from each discussion in turn, until they have completed a full circuit – this will take 54 minutes.*'

Essentially, you are given between five and eight mini interviews, each testing a different skill. Your marks are added up and the total mark helps to assess you. The good news is that even if you fluff one mini interview, the rest could go really well!

Other common types of interview

The marketing interview

One final point. As suggested in the comment from a former admissions tutor at the beginning of the Introduction, many universities invite students to interview before they are made an offer. However, most are marketing interviews. They are designed to persuade you to come to them. Remember, universities are essentially businesses and you are their client. This is not true of those universities that routinely use interviews for all or certain courses (see pages 3–4), BUT it is worth doing some research.

So, should you attend those interviews?
Absolutely! The reason for this is that accepting a place and attending a university is an important step for you. It is expensive and life changing. Therefore, you would be a fool not to have visited the university and spoken to the academics and students in the department before taking the plunge. I am a great believer in informed consent. You can consent to something in an informed way only once you have adequate information.

Selection interviews for university places

These interviews will be a mixture of selection and marketing interviews. Clearly, the applicant wants to get an offer from the university but, on the other hand, if the university sees the applicant as an extremely good candidate, then the university may change the nature of the interview to one in which the professor/interviewer starts to sell the university.

The first part of the interview will be selective but, as the interviewer begins to realise that the candidate is exactly what they want, then the interview will change into a marketing one. The types of questions illustrated in the first section of Chapter Four will be used at the start of the interview, but later on the admissions tutor or professor will begin to 'sell' the college or university by asking soft questions, designed to ascertain what the candidate would like to have at their disposal at the university; this will then be confirmed as available – indeed, the facilities may be very advanced.

> ## TOP TIP
>
> Make some notes shortly after the interview so you can remember what happened. Reflect on what went well, and what could have gone better. Don't feel pressured to share what happened with other people. The interview is between you and your interviewers. Finally, relax and try to forget about this one – it's over!
>
> © The University of Manchester

The format of the standard interview

Opening questions

Why have you applied to this university and college?

This is a nice opening question, designed to put you at your ease. Take time to prepare this answer in advance. Look at the course content. Pick out aspects of the course that you find interesting and prepare to answer the question 'why?' Don't offer a bland or uninteresting response to this question, as it will set the tone for the rest of the interview.

Why have you chosen this course?

As above, this question deserves some pre-interview preparation.

What aspects of your A level course(s) do you enjoy?

Think about the topics that particularly captured your attention. Were these topics that hooked you into the application you are now hoping to secure? What skills have you learnt and how has your academic maturation developed since you completed the GCSE courses?

Have you done any relevant reading? Please discuss.

This is where it is vital that you re-read any texts you mention in the application and prepare additional texts to comment on.

How useful or relevant has your work experience been?

Talk about what you did, why you did it and what you learnt. How did it help you in the decision-making process? Be honest about your experience – if parts of it were eye-opening it will show a maturity in your thinking.

Discuss something you have done of which you are proud.

Think about this and make some notes in advance. If you can, show independent learning, initiative, how you overcame adversity or what positive impact it had on others.

Why should we offer you a place on our course?

This is a bit of an unfair question, but worth preparing for in advance.

Do you have a long-term career goal?

Think about this and if there is nothing you have in mind now, then do say so.

What do you know about the current political issues that affect this profession?

This is a classic medical, health-care or social work question and you are strongly advised to find out from a current practitioner (local GP, social worker, nurse, etc, or even a recent graduate) just what they would say in answer to this question. Read a quality newspaper in the weeks leading up to the interview and any professional journals (BMJ, for instance) that are available online or in the local library.

What positions of responsibility have you held at school?

You may have mentioned that you were a head boy or girl, captain of a sports team or something else in the personal statement. At this point you can show your leadership potential by calmly and carefully showing what you learnt from the position, the challenges you faced and how you overcame them.

What personal qualities do you have?

Sometimes this can be asked in a different way, e.g., what would your friends say are your strengths and weaknesses? Again, prepare an answer in advance and practise it. Be honest – show humility but accentuate the positive and show what you are doing to limit the negative. This is an important question if the course is vocational and you will have contact with people, for instance, education, dentistry, nursing or physiotherapy.

Questions commonly asked at job/apprenticeship interviews

- What attracts you to the idea of completing this scheme rather than going to university?
- What is it about **our** apprenticeship scheme that attracts you?
- Why do you think our scheme matches your qualities?
- What achievement are you most proud of?
- What is your long-term career goal?
- What activities do enjoy outside work/school? Why?

Subjects that should be covered to highlight you as a person:

- teamwork
- leadership
- enthusiasm
- communication skills.

Walk tall, feel confident and remember:

- body language
- voice
- structure your replies to the likely questions from your personal statement/CV.

TIME TO BRAINSTORM: INTERVIEW FORMAT

At this point I recommend that you look at the range of courses and universities that you are applying to and check for the following.

1 Will I be interviewed?
2 Is it a selection or marketing interview?
3 Will I need to prepare a portfolio of work?
4 Will I need to submit written work in advance?
5 Will I be asked to take a test before the interview?
6 Will I be asked to take a test on the day of the interview?

General tips for interviews

All the books will tell you that the interview comprises:

- 80% thinking
- 20% how you project yourself.

Interviewers are impressed 80:20 the other way. In other words, their perception of you is vitally important. Psychologists often call this projection of yourself the 'Big Five Personality Theory'. The following points are therefore essential to successful performance at the interview.

- **Presentation:** The way you physically present yourself will make an impression on an interviewer before you speak. First impressions are critical. It is an unspoken truth that an interviewer makes up their mind within two or three minutes of the start of the interview and spends the rest of the time seeking to confirm their initial decision.
- **Punctuality:** Plan to arrive early; you may be delayed on the way or find it hard to locate the right place. This will give you some preparation and relaxation time.
- **Dress/appearance:** What should I wear? This is a common question that young students ask me. The answer depends on the context. If it is a university interview, then I suggest you wear something that you feel comfortable in. You do not need to wear a jacket and tie, but can if you wish. Do make sure that the clothes you wear are clean and reasonably smart and that your shoes are polished etc. Little things do matter and you do not know what the interviewer is like. Avoid heavy make-up or ostentatious piercings. When you are a student, you can wear what you like, so to compromise now is safe. If the interview is in a business context, then I would recommend a jacket and tie or suitable office clothes.
- **Start of interview:** Remember, the interview starts when the interviewer greets you at the door. At this point the interviewer will be looking at your appearance, your eyes, your response to their greeting, your handshake (no knuckle crunchers or wet-fish handshakes) and possibly your manners. Don't barge past and don't sit down until invited to do so.
- **Smile/eye contact:** Maintain eye contact and avoid irritating or distracting mannerisms. Smile when you first meet the interviewer and when you depart. During the interview smile when the opportunity presents itself. The interviewer is after all human and they will see the funny side of things.
- **Body language:** Sit up, look interested, and it is recommended that you clasp your hands on your knees. Don't cross your arms – this is a defensive position that puts a barrier between you and the interviewer. Don't slide down in the chair. Learn about positive body language. Watch for clues from the interviewer – are they giving you an encouraging nod or looking at their watch?

- **Tone of voice:** Speak at a measured pace. Stress important items by slowing down your delivery and increasing the volume. On the other hand, speed up and reduce volume when the items are less important. Voice variation helps the interviewer to maintain interest.
- **Don't panic:** If you are asked a question you do not understand, then say so. Tutors will not be fazed by you asking for some clarification.
- **Rapport/debate:** In a one-to-one situation, it is important to establish a rapport with the interviewer. Show that you have a mind of your own. You may disagree with the views of the interviewer and this is best expressed by justifying your views with examples to support your case. Interviewers relish the opportunity to debate a subject with an interviewee and if the debate is carried out in the right manner it is usually appreciated.
- **Demonstrate clear thinking:** You need to show that you can think on your feet and respond to different questions that might probe you for greater depth. Be willing to change your position at the end of a debate as this shows that you are not close-minded but open to being influenced.
- **Show passion:** The admissions tutors are in love with their subject (most of the time) and want to teach people and work with people who are equally passionate. Show this with enthusiastic and thoughtful responses to questions.
- **Humour:** Always keep in mind what you are applying for and conduct yourself accordingly. There is nothing wrong with a bit of humour from time to time, but an interview is not the place to be flippant. Avoid being aggressive or arrogant.
- **Waffle/bluff:** Don't waffle or attempt to bluff. If you don't know the answer to the question, admit it openly. Be honest always, thoughtful (there is no problem with a pause before answering a question while collecting your thoughts), unpretentious and enthusiastic.
- **Asking questions:** When invited to ask questions at the end of the interview it is suggested that you limit yourself to two. The answers to these should not be in the university's prospectuses or the company's literature. At the end of the interview thank the interviewer, and if you have enjoyed it, say so. Give the interviewer a final handshake, smile and leave with your head held high.
- **Mobile phone:** Finally, remember to switch off your mobile phone before going into the interview!

HOMEWORK

Read this book and then practise the sample questions with a teacher or friend. Take notes and then think of other questions. Ask for help from former applicants. Students in the year above you or recent leavers may be a source of great help. Do some mock interviews and prepare as thoroughly as you did before making your application.

"I am always amazed at how many people turn up unprepared for an interview. They seem in a state of shock and clearly have not really thought about the sort of questions that they may be asked. Ask for advice in advance, talk to former students, teachers or even just use some common sense. We are not trying to trick you or make you look bad, but do put some time into the preparation to avoid an embarrassing shambling performance. It is an old cliché, but it is true – prepare well or prepare to fail!"

ADMISSIONS TUTOR, IMPERIAL COLLEGE LONDON

TOP TIP

Review your UCAS form, the entry profile and the university prospectus before attending a university interview.

© The University of Manchester

Degree apprenticeships

Many students are now looking at an alternative route, the new degree apprenticeship, which avoids full-time education. Part Three is dedicated to higher and degree apprenticeships.

You would be wise to look at this properly, and there are also many websites to help you. Writing the CV that you submit when you apply to a company for an apprenticeship requires the same care and attention as the personal statement. It must be free of spelling and grammatical errors, and you should avoid colloquial or informal language. You must sell yourself in a way that is compelling and engaging, and shows that you are fully informed about what the apprenticeship will lead to. This is also true of the application letter. It is a formal document, not a text between friends. There is a difference and, in my experience, many teenagers do not understand this.

It is no good being an excellent salesperson at interview if your application form does not lead to an interview. Before an offer of an apprenticeship is made, you will be interviewed. It is at this stage that you will need to sell yourself face to face, because you will be in competition with the other candidates who have also been called to interview.

It is important to stress that the degree apprenticeship is a collaboration between the company and a university. As such, you may be required to complete an application to the company AND an application to the university via UCAS. However, it is the company, not the university, that will conduct the screening interview.

This book will help you to prepare for the interview and give you the appropriate advice on how to succeed, but it will not offer advice about how to write your CV or personal statement.

PART TWO
THE INTERVIEW ITSELF –
SAMPLE QUESTIONS AND
ANSWERS

CHAPTER FOUR
HOW TO PREPARE TO ANSWER TOUGH INTERVIEW QUESTIONS

The advice I have had from all the admissions tutors and students who have undertaken interviews is that there is no such thing as a 'great answer'. They want to hear YOUR answer. That is not to say that you cannot prepare before you attend for interview, and this is what this part of the book focuses on.

The next section starts with a guide on how best to prepare for the classic questions that you will get in an interview. It is not subject specific, but will reference certain subject areas.

The following section will focus on the most popular subjects for which you are *likely to be called for interview in the UK*, based on the most recent UCAS data. Some of the most popular courses are art and design courses, business studies or sports science. You will rarely be interviewed for these, although for the art Foundation course you will have an interview where you discuss your portfolio of work.

The subject-specific information either has been drawn from the universities or – and perhaps most importantly – has come direct from students who I teach who recently attended interviews. I am not trying to offer you a list of perfect answers. I will, however, give you plenty of advice about what sorts of questions to expect and how best to prepare to answer them IN YOUR OWN STYLE. I cannot emphasise this enough. I interview myself and it is very easy to spot the candidate who has stock prepared answers to questions.

The subject-specific section ends with a look at the Oxbridge interview process.

Regarding medicine and Oxbridge, I should point out that this guide provides a foundation for you to understand how to get into these most competitive courses and institutions. There are entire books and websites devoted to this and I will point you in the direction of some useful resources at the ends of those sections.

Answer the question asked

Although this may seem like stating the obvious, always make sure that you're answering the question you've just been asked, and not the questions you've prepared for. I am very wary of the candidate who asks 'What should I say?' and then expects to learn a response like an actor. That would only show the interviewer that you are able to recall information you've already studied or written, rather than provide evidence of your thinking ability (precisely the opposite of what the interview is actually all about).

You need to demonstrate a clear thinking process: tutors want to see that you can analyse a problem and think it through for yourself. It's this sort of skill that will prove invaluable during your time on the course and will determine whether you will complete it successfully or not. If you don't appear motivated, then the tutors won't believe you are committed to the course for the next three or four years. **There is no right answer.**

How to answer the classic interview questions

This section focuses on the common questions that you are likely to be asked, how to prepare to answer them well and what pitfalls to avoid, and gives some inside tips too.

1. Why did you choose this subject?

This is a classic opening question, and is designed to get you to explain your motivation to study the subject. It is very important that your answer sets the right tone. The interviewers are looking for people who can demonstrate a genuine interest in the subject, an awareness of the type of course that they are applying for and its demands, and evidence that you have the basic skills that will enable you to succeed.

WHAT TO SAY

'I have always enjoyed the subject and it plays to my academic strengths.'

Think back to when you chose your A level subjects. You probably chose them because you enjoyed the subject at GCSE. You had a 'natural' flair for the subject and you did not find the lessons boring. The same applies now. If you have studied the subject (sometimes you may not have done), then make your passion and enjoyment plain. You're more likely to be committed and to succeed if you genuinely enjoy the subject you're studying, and you'll probably also be better at the subject.

If you have not studied the subject (for instance you may be applying to read law without ever having studied it), think about the subjects that you enjoy that best fit with the skill base of a law student. Law students must be good at reading, finding arguments in texts, have a good eye for detail, be able to demonstrate independent learning and have good analytical skills.

'Because it fits in perfectly with my career plans.'

Some courses are obviously vocational (for instance, engineering or nursing), but others are not obviously so. In these cases – and a good example is psychology, where many people take the subject with no real intention of practising as a psychologist – it can be a real advantage if you talk intelligently about the course. This is illustrated by this quote:

"I am always impressed when a candidate talks about psychology as a profession. When someone has taken the time to consider, for instance, the difference between clinical, forensic, educational and industrial psychology it sets them apart. In this era of the internet, there is little excuse not to know the difference, at least in essence. It shows an attention to detail and a willingness to go that little step further than the rest."

ADMISSIONS TUTOR, PSYCHOLOGY, DURHAM UNIVERSITY

WHAT *NOT* TO SAY

'To help change the world,' or 'To find a cure for cancer.'

This is a laudable aim but also clichéd.

'My parents always wanted me to apply,' or 'Because my dad is a ...'

Even if this is true, my strong advice is to leave your parents' views out of it! It may be true that your parents want you to study law, medicine or history. However, this will ring alarm bells with admissions tutors as the last thing they want is a reluctant student who is only there because her parents will not support her application to read music! If that rings true with you, it is time for a conversation with your parents about free will and independence.

'Because you earn lots of money.'

Another crass and insensitive response that is likely to alienate you. Remember who you are talking to. They are academics who love their subject – they have not chosen it to finance their first Ferrari. Earning potential is not irrelevant, but naked financial greed will mark you down as a 'Thanks, but no thanks' applicant.

'I liked the university.'

This is a classic trap, particularly when applying to the most competitive of universities. Many students make the mistake of applying to a course that is less competitive (say theology or classics) because they want to go THAT university first and foremost. You must avoid this trap at all costs. This is perfectly illustrated in this quote from an Oxbridge tutor:

> "We still have the student who thinks that 'subject X' will get him into the college, because it is less competitive. What they fail to realise is that many other candidates LOVE subject X and will knock them out of contention when faced with the cold reality of doing it. My advice – apply for the subject you want, not the college!"
>
> **ADMISSIONS TUTOR, OXBRIDGE**

2. Tell me about this claim or book you mention on your personal statement.

The personal statement is the most obvious starting point for a conversation, as you wrote it and the claims you make in it are ones that a good interviewer will want to test. So re-read it and plan for questions on it.

"The personal statement is your opportunity to tell an admissions tutor why you're the right student to be offered a place on their course. We don't interview all our applicants so this is your one chance to sell yourself for courses that don't require an interview. If you do apply to a programme which invites candidates to interview, your personal statement will form the initial basis of your interview."

ADMISSIONS, PLYMOUTH UNIVERSITY

WHAT TO SAY

Clearly, what to say is anything that backs up and substantiates claims made in the statement. This requires some careful forethought.

DO re-read the books and journals you mention, as a bare minimum.

WHAT *NOT* TO SAY

Something that you cannot substantiate.

Something that contradicts your personal statement.

3. What are your academic strengths and weaknesses?

This is another classic question designed to draw you out and see how self-aware or self-effacing you are. Be careful when preparing for this question. There is no reason to pretend that you have no weaknesses. Such a claim is obviously nonsensical. That said, take care to promote your academic strengths and show how you have tried to alleviate the impact of your weaknesses.

WHAT TO SAY ABOUT YOUR WEAKNESSES

'I'm a total perfectionist – I sometimes spend too long agonising over work to get it just right.'

'I spend far too much money on books.'

'I am sometimes outspoken or appear over confident.'

'I do lack confidence in myself at times and it takes me a while to feel that I am genuinely on top of things.'

Do not be afraid to refer to mental health issues, if that is relevant, but only if you feel in control of them now. Also refer to specific learning needs you may have and how you have overcome them. Learning needs are no longer a stigma, so don't hide them.

WHAT *NOT* TO SAY

'I'm just a naturally talented student with no real faults.'

Yes, this is an actual answer from a real student! Their arrogance won them few admirers.

'I find it hard to accept the views of others who are different from me.'

'I am lazy and procrastinate rather than just getting on with things.'

'I am not that good with people.'

Yes again, this is a quote from a potential medic. They were advised to seek a post in a lab setting rather than a hospital ward.

4. Why did you choose this university?

Admissions teams will often use this as an opening question or early conversation starter. It is designed to put you at your ease and explain why you are applying to that institution. They mostly want to know about your interest in the course BUT they also want to understand your motivation for applying. Note the comments in 'What not to say' on page 33 that indicate the person is applying to the university FIRST and the course SECOND.

"We like to know if the person wants to study engineering, not just go to Imperial. One way to find out is to ask, why Imperial?"

ADMISSIONS, IMPERIAL COLLEGE LONDON

Admissions tutors also want to know whether, if they were to offer you a place, you would accept it. Now, in the case of Oxbridge, the answer will very likely be 'yes'. They also want to know that you've done your research, so this question is a good opportunity to demonstrate your knowledge of the university.

WHAT TO SAY

Referring to subject-specific facilities will show that you've done your research.

'Because the course has outstanding employment potential as it is well regarded.'

This is an honest and flattering answer. Admissions tutors know that most students leave academia and get jobs, so that awareness is impressive.

'Your teaching and research reputation is outstanding.'

Again, this is an answer that is both flattering and exposes a depth of research that most students are unwilling to do.

'Because I liked the approach this university takes to my course.'

An awareness of the details of the course at that university is impressive. It shows an attention to detail. Along similar lines, you could also mention the university's great reputation for your subject, or the presence of certain lecturers that you feel inspired by (though don't let this last point dominate your answer; lecturers often move about or go on sabbatical, so even if there's an academic you admire, they may not end up teaching you).

There are many different ranking systems and none is perfect. As with all rankings, the findings need to be taken with some caution. However, an awareness of the rankings will not do you any harm. The two most popular are the QS World University Rankings® and National Student Survey. Both are available online.

The **QS World University Rankings®** are published by British Quacquarelli Symonds annually in September. The universities are compared in four areas of interest – research, teaching, employability and international outlook. Each area of interest is then assessed against six indicators: academic reputation based on a global survey of academics (40%), employer reputation based on a global survey of graduate employers (10%), faculty/student ratio (20%), citations per faculty (20%), international student ratio (5%) and international staff ratio (5%).

The National Student Survey was launched in 2005 and is run by Ipsos MORI. It takes place from January until April each year, with the results published in August. Students at the end of their time at university or college are asked to complete a survey that details what they liked and what could be improved. It aims to help future students by providing information on the quality of courses and encourages institutions to improve the student experience.

Students answer 23 questions relating to six aspects of the learning experience, including teaching on the course, academic support and personal development, plus a question on overall satisfaction. Universities that fail to achieve a 50% response threshold are not included in the results. **The advantage of this survey is that it is only about UK universities.**

"While universities in the Russell Group and some select pre-92 universities perform well according to the raw data, when they are benchmarked against expected performance to take into account factors such as subject mix, entry qualifications and ethnicity (…) a very different picture emerges."
NATIONAL STUDENT SURVEY 2016

John Gill, editor of *Times Higher Education*, said of the last survey that the findings may *'reshape perceptions of university strength'* and challenge *'existing reputations'*.

Use this data to find the BEST COURSE and prepare for the TOUGH interview!

WHAT *NOT* TO SAY

'For the nightlife.'

This shows that you're motivated by the wrong things. University is primarily about studying, not about partying the night away, and answering this question in this way may raise alarm bells, making interviewers question whether you'd be committed to your studies. You could say, **'It has a great location'** instead.

'Because it was cheaper than the others I looked at.'

Even if this was one of your reasons, it's best not to mention it; although finance is an understandable concern, it's better to focus your answer on the course.

'Because my parents are alumni.'

Keep parents or relations out of it! The only exception to that would be to mention a sibling at the college or university who spoke highly of their experience. That may be relevant, particularly if they did well. Best to avoid, though, if they were rarely seen in the library!

5. What are you reading now?

That is not a trick question. Clearly, if you are an English literature student you may wish to think harder than usual. However, if not, they are probably hoping that you answer either with a book that is loosely relevant to the course or, if not, something that is 'good'.

Questions like this or, more simply, 'what are you reading now that relates to your A level courses?' are designed to spark discussion as well as to test what you read beyond the confines of the A level syllabus. Be prepared to answer questions about whatever you mention here.

WHAT TO SAY

Mention a book that has relevance and that you have READ! Please do not lie at this stage.

For scientists, a reputable publication such as *Nature, Scientific American* or *New Scientist* would be acceptable, providing that you can talk about specific articles or discoveries that interested you.

For non-English subjects, you could mention a work of fiction if it's highly relevant and you think they're likely to have read it – e.g. *Pompeii* by Robert Harris if you're applying for a classical archaeology subject (this would spark discussion of historical accuracy).

You could mention a decent newspaper. Be prepared to talk about current affairs, even if just briefly. They want students with more awareness than just the latest iPhone or Instagram update.

WHAT *NOT* TO SAY

Anything that is not true. I once sat in on an interview at a medical school where the candidate claimed to have read an article in *Nature*. The interviewer was the author. The interviewee had not read it. Cue – mortal embarrassment all round.

'Nothing! I don't read much.'

An irrelevant novel, magazine or second-rate newspaper.

6. What can you bring to the department or university?

This question is asking about what qualities, other than academic, you can contribute. It is a very common question. In answering it, think about the extracurricular interests you have, the skills you possess other than academic and your positive personal traits. They are choosing to have you in their classroom, tutorial or common rooms.

Avoid humorous or overly self-aggrandising answers here; instead, focus on selling yourself (modestly) to the interviewer and highlighting the key traits that make you a good person to have around. Support what you say with concrete examples of your experience. Think about how you currently contribute to your school or college, and how your activities might be applied to a university environment.

For instance, if you are head of the debating society at school, what skills or qualities do you possess that would allow you to be a successful member of the university's debating society, or any other club/team you might wish to join there?

WHAT TO SAY

'As an enthusiastic member of my school debating society, I enjoy academic debate, so I think I'd be able to contribute a lot to class discussions.'

'I would consider myself to be a good sportsman or woman and would be delighted to play for the college, department or university.'

'I have experience of leadership at school, of showing initiative and starting projects.'

Clearly, in this case you will need to have examples to back up your claims.

'I am a published writer, poet, playwright, journalist ...'

Again, have examples, where appropriate. By 'published', you do not mean 'you can find my stuff in Waterstones'! You could be published online, in a school magazine or as a competition entry winner.

WHAT *NOT* TO SAY

Anything that you cannot substantiate with evidence.

Anything that makes you appear socially inept, arrogant or overly confident.

7. What work experience have you done? What did it teach you?

This is a crucial question if you are applying for a course that has clear vocational aims. The obvious examples are medicine, dentistry, nursing, physiotherapy, speech therapy, veterinary medicine and NHS-based occupations with degree routes. You may also be asked this if you are applying for a course with qualified teacher status (QTS), where you will need to show an awareness of current trends in education.

The **Medical School at the University of Sheffield** explains that relevant work experience helps students to develop their medical knowledge and skills, and ensures that they have *'an understanding of the complex nature of a doctor's role, as well as being aware of the highs and lows of the profession'*.

The NHS Careers website refers directly to the importance of work experience: *'Try to get as much experience as you feasibly can; start gaining it as early as you can. What you want to make sure of is that you have something that you can talk about on your personal statement and at interview.'*

Work placements are not normally an entry requirement for those hoping to take a humanities course, though they may help a candidate stand out.

Mary Beard, Professor of Classics at the University of Cambridge, says: *'Work experience is one of the things that can give me some idea of how a student can reflect analytically on a new experience.'* But she adds that simply listing where you have completed work placements isn't enough: *'However glamorous or enterprising it was, if a student can't reflect thoughtfully on it – well that counts against them.'*

This last point is very important. It is not the experience that counts as much as its relevance, how it helped to shape your understanding of the course, how it helped you to better understand the profession and what skills you learnt that are transferable.

WHAT TO SAY

Subject-specific work experience is ideal; you can then say things like **'It taught me that this is definitely the career I want to pursue,'** or **'It gave me an insight into the challenges of the profession.'** Mention conversations with other professionals, the things that you DID, not just observed, and how these skills are transferable.

Once again, Mary Beard puts it well: *'I'm interested in work experience only to the extent that the applicant has something intellectually interesting to say about it.'*

Another possible good answer is:

'I spent the summer working as a personal assistant to a researcher in a research and development lab, which taught me to be very organised. It also gave me a unique insight into how academia can be applied to the real world.'

WHAT *NOT* TO SAY

That you did not learn much from the experience.

Anything that you cannot substantiate – don't lie, in other words.

Any work experience that has no bearing on the application. Your time in the local café is not relevant unless you can show that it taught you important customer service skills, you ended up managing shifts or something else.

8. What achievement are you most proud of?

This is another chance to highlight your suitability for and interest in the course, so try to make it subject relevant if possible.

WHAT TO SAY

'I felt proud to be awarded first place in a poetry competition with a sonnet I wrote about ...' (If you're applying for English.)

'I entered an essay for a university or national competition.'

There are many of these, so go online and look for one in your subject. Even entering will set you apart.

'I led a successful campaign to do ... or set up a new ...'

Admissions tutors like initiative, leadership, independence and the ability to get something done.

'I recently won the Senior Challenge for the UK Mathematics Trust.'

You should enter such competitions. An entry alone gives weight to an application.

'I won an academic scholarship for my subject at school or a prize for outstanding achievement.'

WHAT *NOT* TO SAY

Something that is irrelevant to the course or is overtly humorous. Humour is a dangerous thing at interview, so keep your comments serious for now. There will be plenty of time to show off the one-liners when you enter the college stand-up comedian competition. Interestingly, I have taught two very well-known stand-ups in my time – neither was that funny or interested in stand-up at school!

9. Why should we offer you a place?

This is the obvious, final question. It is designed to see what you can say to add value to your application. Competition is fierce, so make sure that you have considered your answer to this question carefully.

My advice is to say something non-controversial, and lighthearted too, if appropriate.

Focus on the skills you have, your passions and your ambitions. If this question comes last, it's probably designed to wrap up the interview.

WHAT TO SAY

This is a good opportunity to recap what you've highlighted already – your strengths, career aims, what you can contribute and so on.

At the very end, if you judge that the interviewers would respond well, you could also lighten the tone and end on a note that injects some of your personality, by saying (with a grin) something like *'Also, I'm told I bake a good cake so tutorials would be fun!'*

WHAT *NOT* TO SAY

'Because I'm worth it.'

Nicking a good line from a well-known shampoo advert is a bit crass.

'Because I am better than all the other applicants.'

Undermining your fellow applicants is ungracious and appears arrogant, particularly from a teenager!

---

10. Is there anything that you would like to ask?

Do expect this as a final interview question. It is not a trick one and your application does not hinge on the answer. It is worth thinking about one or two questions in advance that you might ask. It shows that you are interested.

WHAT TO SAY

'What are the career prospects for a graduate from your department?'

'How many students stay on to complete postgraduate research?'

'What student support arrangements are in place to support my learning needs?'

Clearly, this is relevant if you have indicated such a need on your UCAS form. By the way, as I have stated before, this is not a stigma, so be honest.

'Do you offer any scholarships or bursaries?'

WHAT *NOT* TO SAY

Do not ask about anything that is obvious from reading the prospectus. If you have nothing to say of note, avoid saying anything other than perhaps, **'No, I think you have answered all my questions and thank you for interviewing me.'**

NOTE: How you leave the room is important. THANK the interviewers, smile, shake hands and say how you hope to hear from them. If you enjoyed the conversation, say so!

Activity: STAR Method

The STAR method can be a good way of answering questions, allowing you to evidence situations that have enabled you to develop the skills and experiences relevant to your chosen course.

Situation: What was the situation? Give the interviewer a brief outline of the situation faced and your role.

Task: What were the main issues involved with the situation?

What needed to be done?

Action: What task/s needed to be achieved and what was the desired outcome?

What obstacles had to be overcome?

Result: What was the outcome?

Why not try for yourself? We have given an example to help. The student below is applying for English and Drama.

Question	Can you tell us something about how you organise your time when you are studying?
Situation	*Attending Sixth Form College and having a weekend job in a clothes shop.*
Task	*Complete my A' level coursework on time and attend my weekend job where I am responsible for ordering stock and serving customers.*
Action	*Manage my time effectively to leave enough time to complete my school work, whilst also working hard at my weekend job ensuring I complete the tasks I am responsible for.*
Result	*By doing this part time job I have developed good communication skills, the ability to manage my time well and have taken on levels of responsibility. This will help with my English and Drama degree, as I have experience of managing my workload successfully and will work well with my fellow students in the team work activities that are required as part of the degree.*

Question	Have you completed a project or some other study by yourself? What was good and bad about this?
Situation	
Task	
Action	
Result	

Question	Can you give an example of a time when you have worked with others to complete an activity? What did you like the most/least about this?
Situation	
Task	
Action	
Result	

Question	Can you give us an example of when you had to have something ready for a certain date? How did you organise your time to make sure you met the deadline?
Situation	
Task	
Action	
Result	

CHAPTER FIVE
SUBJECT-SPECIFIC ADVICE

In this section I have chosen several subjects where applicants are commonly interviewed with some detailed guidance on how you might prepare. I have offered some guidance about how you might approach some of the questions and then suggested a few more questions to practise as part of the preparation process. This practice is very important and something that I suggest you do in the run up to the interview. It is very important to look at the relevant university websites for more examples. Oxford and Cambridge do prepare many and I am grateful to them for allowing me to reproduce some in this publication. You can also get hold of some useful books and some of these will be referred to later in this section.

Once again, let me emphasise that it is important to think about YOUR answers to these questions and not just learn a stock answer from this book.

I also suggest some additional reading that might help you prepare and good websites for up-to-date information.

The order of this section is as follows.

- Biological sciences
- Business management and economics
- Education – Postgraduate Certificate in Education (PGCE)
- Engineering
- Medicine and dentistry
- Nursing and midwifery
- Occupational therapy and radiotherapy
- Performing and creative arts – drama, music and art
- Physiotherapy
- Social work
- Veterinary medicine
- Oxbridge interviews

Biological sciences

What are biological sciences?

Biological sciences is a broad-based degree course that can cover many topics ranging from cell and molecular biology to genetics, marine and freshwater biology, biodiversity and applied ecology. Most biological sciences degrees will provide a broad and balanced knowledge of modern biology, centred on the organism but including molecular, genetic, cellular and population aspects, and the opportunity to specialise. Biological sciences courses will cover field and laboratory skills and training in scientific methods as well as theoretical knowledge.

Applicants should be able to demonstrate a firm knowledge and serious interest in biology and issues related to the subject such as stem cell therapy, vaccines, conservation, evolution and climate change. As biological sciences is such a large area of study that covers many topics, universities tend to offer the opportunity to specialise within the course. Therefore, if an applicant can express an interest in a certain area of biology, this can be advantageous.

"The Biological Sciences BSc offers you an extremely wide choice of optional modules ranging from molecular genetics to behaviour and ecology, and a flexible programme of study."
UNIVERSITY COLLEGE LONDON

Background to the course

Biological sciences courses come either as single honours courses or as part of a joint honours degree and are very diverse. The core strands that unite all the various disciplines and sub-disciplines of the subject are the study and characterisation of living organisms and the investigation of the science of living things. This means most biology courses will have core modules focusing on subjects such as cell theory and molecular biology, evolution, physiology and adaptation, gene theory, and homeostasis. Later options could include environmental biology, forensic biology, genetics, marine biology, microbiology, molecular biosciences, natural science, neurobiology, physiology, zoology and many others.

Most courses will teach you key transferable skills including how to manage and use laboratory equipment, statistical analysis, how to draw conclusions from diverse data sets, how to present findings orally and how to work well in teams, collaborating with people who have different skill sets. These are all important for the workplace and hence desired by employers.

Interview format and outline

The vast majority of interviews for biological sciences will be a one-to-one, panel or small group interview. They may last anything from 15 to 30 minutes and will comprise questions to assess your motivation to study, your personal statement and your academic potential.

Sample questions

All the following sample questions and answers come from the University of Oxford. I am grateful for permission to publish them. You can also see new and updated questions online at: www.ox.ac.uk/admissions/undergraduate/applying-to-oxford/interviews/sample-interview-questions.

Why do some habitats support higher biodiversity than others?

This question encourages students to think about what high-diversity habitats such as rainforests and coral reefs have in common. In many cases, patterns or correlations can help us to identify the underlying mechanisms. For example, a student might point out that both rainforests and coral reefs are found in hot countries and near the equator. The best answers will attempt to unravel exactly what it is about being hot or near the equator that might allow numerous types of plant and animal to arise, persist and coexist. Do new species evolve more frequently there, or go extinct less frequently? Once students have come up with a plausible theory, I'd follow up by asking them how they would go about testing their idea. What sort of data would they need?

Why do many animals have stripes?

The main aim of the question is to get applicants to think about biological topics and put them in the context of successful adaptations to life on earth. So I might expect students to start by thinking of some stripy animals, then move on to thinking about categories of striped animals – for example, those that are dangerous (such as wasps, tigers and snakes), those that have stripes for camouflage (such as zebras and tigers) and those whose stripes are harmless mimics of dangerous ones. They might think of specific examples for detailed comparison: tigers and zebras for example both have stripes for camouflage and blending in with background, one to hide from prey and the other to hide from predators.

Other things that would be worth considering include whether stripes may only occur in the young of a species; whether the colour of the stripes matters rather than just the contrasting stripe pattern; and why do stripe size, shape, width and pattern vary in different species. There are no right or wrong specific answers to the questions – I'm just interested in candidates' speculations about the advantages of having stripes.

Here's a cactus. Tell me about it.

We wouldn't actually phrase the question this way – we give the student a cactus in a pot and a close-up photo of the cactus's surface structure and ask them to describe the object in as much detail as possible using the plant and the photo. We are looking for observation and attention to detail, both at the large and micro scale. We ask them to account for what they see – this means they don't have to use memory or knowledge about cacti (even if they have it) but to deduce the uses and functions of the shapes, sizes, structures that they have just described. So, for example, why be fat and bulbous? Or, why have large sharp spines, surrounded by lots of very small hair-like spines? Why does it have small cacti budding off the main body? There will frequently be more than one logical answer to these questions, and we are likely to follow one answer with another question – for example: 'The big spines are to stop the cactus being eaten, yes, but by what sort of animals?' We would also bring in more general questions at the end of the cactus discussion, such as what are the problems faced by plants and animals living in very dry habitats such as deserts?

If you could save either the rainforests or the coral reefs, which would you choose?

I'd expect students to be able to use their general knowledge plus their common sense to come up with an answer – no detailed knowledge is required. Students might then be asked about the importance of natural features, such as biodiversity and rare species, and human interests, such as the fuel and food, ecotourism and medicines we get from rainforests or reefs. Finally, there are impacts to consider from climate change, soil erosion, pollution, logging, biofuel replacement, overfishing, etc. The final answer doesn't matter – both reefs and rainforests must be managed sustainably to balance conservation and human needs.

Is it easier for organisms to live in the sea or on land?

Firstly, candidates should define 'easier' – does it mean less complexity, less energy expenditure, less highly evolved, less likely to be eaten, etc.? Then candidates could think of problems caused by living in the sea, such as high salinity, high pressure, lack of light, etc. Problems living on land include extra support for the body, avoiding desiccation, the need for more complex locomotor systems (legs, wings, etc.) and hence better sensory and nervous systems. Then ask in which of the two ecosystems have animals and plants been more successful? So now they should define 'successful'.

Why do lions have manes?

Some of the best interview questions do not have a right or a wrong answer, and can potentially lead off in all sorts of different directions. Applicants might have picked up ideas about the function of a lion's mane from independent reading or from watching natural history documentaries. That's fine – but I'd follow up their response by asking how they would test their theory. When I've used this question in interviews I've had all sorts of innovative suggestions, including experiments where lions have their manes shaved to investigate whether this influences their chances with the opposite sex or helps them win fights over territory.

Ladybirds are red. So are strawberries. Why?

Many biological sciences tutors use plant or animal specimens – often alive – as a starting point for questions and discussion, so applicants shouldn't be surprised if they are asked to inspect and discuss an insect or a fruit. Red can signal either 'don't eat me' or 'eat me' to consumers. I'm interested in seeing how applicants attempt to resolve this apparent paradox.

Would it matter if tigers became extinct?

This question is not about hoping students will display their expert knowledge of tigers. Most applicants would instinctively answer 'Yes ...', but it is the 'because ...' that interests me, and can help to distinguish critical thinkers. I might follow up this question by asking if it would matter if less glamorous creatures – like fungi – became extinct.

Other common questions

- What part of the biology A level course did you enjoy the most?
- What part did you find the least inspiring? Why?
- How do you see your study of biology fitting in with your future career?
- What ethical dilemmas are there in the use of stem cells for research?
- What is DNA?
- Describe the ways in which water and the regulation of water content are important to organisms.
- Describe how nucleotides, molecules that derive from nucleotides and nucleic acids, are important in keeping organisms alive.
- Explain the ethical implications of genetic modification.

RECOMMENDED READING

- Biochemical Society: www.biochemistry.org
- British Ecological Society: www.britishecologicalsociety.org
- Royal Society of Biology: www.rsb.org.uk for links to careers advice.
- The Royal Society: https://royalsociety.org – follow the Science Issues link.

TOP TIP

Listen really carefully to the question, and take time to think about your answer. Answer the one you have been asked, not the one you wish you had. If you get tangled up, say so and start again.

© The University of Manchester

Business, management and economics

What is business and management?

The practice of business and management (and all the other specialisms, such as accounting, marketing and economics) is a varied and fascinating subject and taking place around us every day. The globalised business and financial world and the power of brands, finance, marketing, consumer behaviour, large organisations and multinationals, along with the importance of entrepreneurship and forward thinking, mean that a business degree is useful in many careers. Many business degrees include a fantastic opportunity to take a placement year in industry/commerce or to work or study abroad as part of the course. Business students are a massively varied group of people, often from all over the world, offering lots of new perspectives, friends and future contacts.

....

"We pride ourselves on nurturing business-ready minds and developing graduates who can do. Some of this you can't learn in the classroom – you have to learn by doing."
ADMISSIONS, UNIVERSITY OF SURREY

What is economics?

Economics is not all about money. It is a people-focused subject. It is also highly diverse, with many combinations available. It is a social science and covers all the key parts of this area, including psychology, law, geography, ethics, politics, history and sociology. Most courses expect a sound knowledge of maths – many require Maths A level or equivalent. Economics can be combined with many other subjects, including maths and, perhaps most famously, politics and philosophy to make PPE.

Microeconomics looks at the behaviour and interactions of agents – such as households, small and large companies, and buyers and sellers. Macroeconomics looks at the overarching policies set by governments – including tax policy, inflation, monetary growth and the causes of unemployment.

Background to the courses

Courses in economics and business management are very popular and account for some of the most oversubscribed courses at UK universities. Many students are drawn to the prospect of high earnings in banking after graduation. While this is realistic, it is also important to know that such prestige jobs are also highly competitive! You will need first-class qualifications and excellent people skills to succeed in the recruitment process. Many others, of course, use business and economics degrees as a springboard for a career in other sectors, including all forms of business, law, accountancy, marketing and teaching.

The term 'business degree' covers a range of courses and they are often called different names. They are very often combined honours courses and many students will study business with another course, including languages, law, accountancy or marketing. Most courses last three years, although some have four-year options with work placements or overseas placements for high-achieving students. This is something to think about when applying. Business degrees are usually assessed using a combination of coursework and examinations, and the teaching process often involves a strong focus on case studies. Many transferable skills are learnt, including numeracy, IT proficiency, time management, presentation skills and data set analysis.

Economics is a more specialist field and most economics degrees today require a high mathematical competency. The transferable skills are similar to those of business courses although the specialist nature of the course does mean that you will be most attractive to banking or corporate businesses that are seeking candidates with a bespoke skill set.

Interview format and outline

Most interviews will be one to one or panel. You will be quizzed on your motivation to study and your personal statement and you will be asked questions that will assess your academic potential. Expect to be asked to solve a numerical question if you are applying for a course with a strong maths component.

Sample questions

What are the key issues in the world of business now?

"We need to see evidence of commitment to a business and management degree, for instance a demonstrable interest in the business world. A good candidate would have an awareness of recent issues in the UK economy that are relevant, for instance the recent upheaval in the sub-prime market and its impact on banking and finance."

BRUNEL UNIVERSITY

A good candidate will show an awareness of globalisation, customer focus, organisations and how they work, the importance of brands and marketing, finance and economics. A candidate interested in banking and finance would need to put forward a case as to why they want to specialise at this stage. There is no reason not to, but this ambition needs to be explained – to make money is not a good response!

What skills do you think you need to succeed in this course?

Again, Brunel University refers to a few key skills – numeracy, good communication and teamwork skills. Your answer should show evidence of leadership or putting forward new ideas – for example, part-time or voluntary work. Initiative is rewarded, so show evidence of projects you have set up, such as student magazines or student-led fundraising schemes. The Young Enterprise and Duke of Edinburgh's Award schemes are other means of showing these attributes.

Do bankers deserve the pay they receive? And should the government do something to limit how much they get?

This refers to the financial crisis of 2008. A simple answer might be that since banks are generally private firms and workers are free to work where they wish, then the pay they receive is just the outcome of a competitive labour market. In this story, bankers earn a lot because they are very skilled and have rare talents. It is hard to see a reason for government intervention in this case – though on equity grounds you might want to have a progressive income tax system that redistributes some of this income. A good candidate would wonder why it is that seemingly equally talented people can get paid so much more in banking than in other occupations. Do we really believe that bankers are so much better than other workers in terms of skill? An alternative story is that the banking industry is not competitive and generates profits above what a competitive market would produce. This would then also allow workers in that industry to share some of those profits and so earn much more. In this case, there is a role for government intervention – making the market more competitive. The key point about this question is to try to get candidates to think about the economics of pay rather than just whether they think it is fair or not.

(An answer from the University of Oxford)

The holiday puzzle

Alex and Brian are planning a four-day holiday in Venice and each have 400 euros to spend. (They have already paid for their return flights and hotel room.) On the flight out Alex and Brian discuss how they should each allocate their spending over the four days.

Alex believes that the satisfaction he gains from spending a certain amount, x euros, on a given day is proportional to $\sqrt{x}$. Explain why this might be a reasonable way to represent his preferences. If Alex has these preferences, how would you expect him to allocate his spending over the four days?

Brian has the same preferences as Alex, but he knows that he tends to be impatient. This means that, on any given day, he tends to give extra weight to the current day's spending when he makes his spending decisions for that day. Thus, on a given day he behaves as if the satisfaction he would gain from spending x euros would be $\sqrt{(2x)}$, whereas he thinks that on subsequent days the satisfaction he will gain from spending x euros will be only $\sqrt{x}$. If Brian has these preferences how would you expect him to allocate his spending over the four days?

Is there a better way for Brian to allocate his spending and, if so, how might he achieve this better outcome?

Does your analysis of this problem have implications for current economic policy issues?

After asking one or two general questions such as 'What topic in economics have you enjoyed most, or found most surprising?' we move on to working through a puzzle. We give the candidate a copy 10 minutes before the interview starts. We might spend 10–15 minutes going through the implications of the puzzle during the interview, though this depends on how far candidates get, and how quickly they get there!

Each puzzle is designed to see how willing candidates are to abstract from the complexities of a real world case involving some economic principles and to put such principles to work. There are usually some simple mathematical ideas involved (in this case, the idea that the utility function provided implies that it is best to allocate spending uniformly over the four days). However, we do not expect any calculations to be performed, though drawing a diagram is often useful (as it is in this example).

(An answer from an Oxbridge admissions tutor)

Why is income per head between 50 and 100 times larger in the United States than in countries such as Burundi and Malawi?

The question is focused on perhaps the most important economic question there is: why are some countries rich and some countries poor? As with most economics questions, there is no simple or unique answer. Candidates need to think about all the potential reasons why such income gaps exist. A good starting point is to think about whether the amount of capital and technology available to workers in different countries is the same, and if not, why not? US workers are much more productive because they have access to the best technology – the US is at the technological frontier. But why do poor countries not just buy the same technology and be as productive? Possibly, the education levels are too low to allow for the use of such technology, or perhaps there are insufficient savings to purchase the technology or the infrastructure might not exist. Good candidates should recognise that institutions matter a lot – respect for property rights and the rule of law appear to be prerequisites for sustainable development. Other factors might include trade restrictions by the rich world on poor countries' exports, civil wars, disease (e.g. AIDS, malaria), etc. The trick is to think widely and not to try to fit the answer to some lesson that has been learnt in school.

(An answer from an Oxbridge admissions tutor)

Other common questions

- Many non-economists are inclined to blame economics for the mess we're in – are they right?
- Should the Bank of England now start to raise interest rates in a bid to boost aggregate demand?
- Interest rates – or yields – on 10-year bonds issued by the UK government are at their lowest level since 1703. Over the summer, yields on German and Swiss two-year bonds turned negative. What explains such low bond yields?
- What is the difference between a leader and a manager?
- Small is beautiful, but it is also efficient – why are governments and businesses so obsessed by economies of scale?
- To help recovery, the focus should be on debt and leverage in the economy and turning instead to equity financing. Discuss.
- In the long run, bailing out people is less harmful to the economy than bailing out businesses. Discuss.

- Who are the principal beneficiaries of innovation? Inventors? Shareholders? Or consumers?
- Despite a deep downturn, corporate insolvencies have remained remarkably low in recent years – is good management the reason?

RECOMMENDED READING

- McGrath, Michael, *Getting into Business & Economics Courses*, Trotman Education, 2017
- *The Economist*
- *Financial Times*
- *The Spectator*

Education – Postgraduate Certificate in Education (PGCE)

What is a PGCE?

The PGCE is a course that allows you to teach in the UK. You can teach in the infant or primary sector (normally Foundation Year to Year 6) or in the secondary sector (Year 7 to Year 13). Teaching is a rewarding and demanding career that is better paid than many people think.

When thinking about a career in this sector, think carefully about your skills and attributes. **Good teachers tend to be passionate about their subject.** They pass on this interest to their students. This is particularly true in the secondary sector, where I think we can all remember good teachers who made lessons interesting and showed a genuine interest in the subject that rubbed off on you.

Teachers also need to be **great communicators**. Teaching is like acting, in that for much of the time you are performing! You need to be able to hold the attention of children, who will test your patience from time to time, and you also need to be able to communicate well on paper, too, as report writing and essay marking are part of the job. You will also meet parents, who have a whole different dynamic and can be supportive, hostile or just plain ignorant about their children! This makes each day different, but it is not a job that will suit you if team working, unpredictability, a certain amount of stress and personal energy are not for you.

You must also be willing to **shoulder responsibility**. Teaching is both intellectually and emotionally demanding. You need to be **capable of dealing with poor behaviour**, keeping up with marking and paperwork, **handling stress** and taking a **caring**, responsible approach to your pupils' problems. You will get plenty of support, but in the end, the classroom is your domain and you must own it. Good teachers are also **self-aware and self-critical** – they reflect on what they have done and look to make it better. They must have a **sense of humour**, be willing to work in the evenings from time to time and, finally and most importantly, **they must like children**! Too many teachers I have met just don't really like children.

When you are interviewed ALL the above will be highlighted and assessed.

Background to the course

Although some undergraduate degrees in the UK have 'education' in the title, this profile will focus on the most common route into primary or secondary education in the UK. This is through the PGCE, which gives the holder qualified teacher status (QTS) once they complete the newly qualified teacher (NQT) year. The independent (private) sector does not always expect teachers to hold a PGCE – however, many do, and all state schools expect their teachers to have QTS. You can specialise as a primary or secondary school teacher too.

This profile will briefly outline what is required to be accepted into the teaching profession, what grants and bursaries are available to support you and, finally, what to expect at an interview. The majority of universities that offer the PGCE will interview applicants to assess their suitability to work with children.

The first decision to make is whether you want to undertake **school-led training** or **university-led training**. The latter is a newer process but one that is growing in popularity. If your preference is to be based at a school and you want hands-on experience at a school from day one, then the school-led training route is for you. If, however, you want to go to college or university first to learn the pedagogy of teaching before you apply it in a work placement, then the university-led route is better for you. They are different approaches that suit different people, but both lead the same outcome – a PGCE and QTS.

There are other exceptions to look at too. One is the **Teach First Programme**. This is aimed at graduates with a 1st class or 2.1 degree. This pays you a salary while on the training programme and is school led. For more details, search online for Teach First. Other routes include the **Researchers in Schools** route, which specialises in helping applicants completing their PhD to become teachers, and the **Troops for Teachers** programme, which is designed to help former members of the armed services qualify for teaching posts. Finally, there are the **Future Teaching Scholarship** – money to help you if you are training to become **a maths or physics teacher** – and the **Assessment only route**, for those who have experience as teachers but did not complete a PGCE. Details of all these programmes can be found online.

Before you apply it is important that you understand the minimum standards that the government requires for you to be eligible to start the course. This applies specifically to the most common routes into education – the school-led and the university-led PGCE. The other programmes have subtly different eligibility.

- All applicants must have a C/4 grade (B grade in Wales) in English and Maths GCSE (or equivalent). This applies whether you join a primary or secondary teaching route.
- If you do not have the above, you will be asked to pass a GCSE equivalency test BEFORE you are interviewed. You can find more about this online or by speaking to a university.
- You will need a degree to acquire QTS. Overseas degrees from both inside and outside the EU may count too, but you must discuss this with the school or university first to check eligibility.

◗ Most secondary school teachers have a degree in a subject that they would expect to teach up to A level. However, this is not always the case and you can easily teach maths (for instance) if you have a good degree in economics or engineering OR you can teach English with a joint honours degree in philosophy and English. Employers in top schools will, however, look to recruit teachers with the best qualifications in the target subjects. To that end, you will do well if you have an MA or higher when applying for jobs.

◗ There are also routes into teaching for those without a degree – these are restricted to the university-led undergraduate course route, where the bachelor's degree will have QTS built in. There are two types of degree that lead to QTS, both of which tend to focus on primary school placements, although there are secondary-level options available:

- Bachelor of Education (BEd)
- Bachelor of Arts (BA) and Bachelor of Science (BSc) with QTS.

◗ These courses generally require three to four years' full-time study, depending on the number and length of your school placements. Some can take two years if you already have undergraduate credits from previous studies. You apply for these courses through UCAS.

The UK government has a helpful website called Get Into Teaching (https://getintoteaching. education.gov.uk) aimed at potential teachers, which is well worth a visit. It also operates a good mentoring service, where experienced teaching professionals offer online advice to potential applicants. The site also has details of the bursaries and scholarships available.

Interview format and outline

It is important to prepare well before you apply. Your application will not be successful if you do not take this process seriously. One of the most important things you need to do – and this is something that will be drawn out in an interview – is to gain relevant work experience. Spending time in schools shadowing teachers will help you to make an informed choice about teaching. Contact a local school, or even your former school, and talk to them about coming in for a few sessions.

When asking to arrange work experience, do your homework. Contact different types of school – small, large, rural, urban, faith schools, community colleges, grammar schools and prep schools. This list is long and you do not have to visit each type BUT it is sometimes much better to be able to talk about the RANGE of schools you visited than just one or two. Find out about each school and write a letter to the head teacher that is *not generic*, but talks about *their* school and why you want to visit it. They are likely to be more interested in your application if you say that you specifically chose their school because it was so good! You will also have to be flexible and cooperate with the schools to make it work for both of you.

You can also do other volunteer work that helps your application. This could include working with children in a church or faith setting, in an after-school club, in a scouts group or in a youth club. Most of these schools and clubs will ask you to complete the Disclosure and Barring Service (DBS) form. This is a 'police' check and may take a few weeks, so be patient.

All applicants who want to work with children will need to have employment eligibility (visa or work permits if you are not a UK national). You will also need to undertake the DBS check before you start the school placement or university course. Many universities also operate a 'fitness to train' scheme. This requires applicants to some courses, including all PGCE courses, to pass health assessments. One such university is **Goldsmiths, University of London**. It requests that you complete an occupational health form designed to make sure that:

- your health will not be compromised by your profession (any existing health problems will not become worse)
- the health and safety of other staff will not be adversely affected by your being unfit to work
- everyone – including people with disabilities – who wants to work in teaching or social work can achieve their potential through reasonable adjustments, if necessary. The college will make adjustments, including making sure that placements are accessible.

The interview and selection process will depend on the type of application you have made. Some will keep you busy for most of the day. However, others will be over in an hour, with a one-to-one interview and a short tour.

It is important that you do your research before you go, as no two colleges, schools or universities run exactly the same process. The types of assessments and interviews that you could expect include:

- a review of personal documentation, including examination certificates
- a group task or discussion (e.g. conversation on current educational issues)
- a short presentation – the topic may be given to you before the day of the interview
- an individual interview, which could be on a one-to-one basis or with a panel
- a written task, or tasks, which could involve a literacy test and/or subject-based test.

Goldsmiths makes it clear that *'There is no single model of the "ideal" applicant, and applications are considered on their individual merits. We are looking for people with a genuine interest in – and enthusiasm for – teaching, and aptitude for working with young people and engaging them in learning. This can be demonstrated in several different ways:*

- *through experience of activities with young people outside school*
- *evidence of continued interest in your subject*
- *evidence of the ability to interact and communicate successfully with a range of people*
- *evidence of the ability to organise and manage your time effectively.'*

Sample questions

The answers to the questions that follow have been provided by interviewers. I am grateful to the Get Into Teaching website (https://getintcteaching.education.gov.uk) for allowing me to reproduce these.

What challenges do you anticipate facing as a trainee and what strategies will you employ to help you overcome them?

"Answers will ideally show a realistic idea of what the training course will involve, and of the demands of working in a school plus the additional demands from university, such as written assignments. Answers should also give a sense of trying to manage work-life balance and having interests outside of training to provide that balance. Answers may also relate to talking to their mentor, course tutor, departmental colleagues and peers to find the help and support they need."

PAUL BAINBRIDGE, ASSOCIATE ASSISTANT HEAD TEACHER, BURNHAM GRAMMAR SCHOOL

Can you explain an instance when you have been offered constructive criticism and describe how you acted upon it?

"I'd be looking for an applicant to display a positive attitude towards advice and constructive criticism offered by colleagues, regardless of their colleague's age, seniority or level of experience. I'd be looking for a specific and detailed example of how the trainee was able to take the feedback on board and carry out the suggested improvements, as well as an understanding of the impact of these changes on the quality of their work. This question enables us to recruit applicants who will be committed to their own professional development, share the positive values we promote within the partnership and who will be able to meet Standard 8 (8d) of the Teachers' Standards."

HELEN BYRON, HEAD OF TRAINING, BURTON MEADOW ITTC

Why do you want to teach?

"There are lots of different answers to this, but the best answers are always when the trainee gives a very specific example from a positive or challenging experience they have had already. Real-life examples are so much better than 'I want to make a difference'."

DARREN PRIESTLEY, ASSISTANT HEAD TEACHER, ANGLO EUROPEAN SCHOOL

What are the current issues in education today?

"The response to this can be anything, but this is a question which on the whole is answered very poorly. Reading the TES (Times Educational Supplement), educational blogs or journals will provide a host of key issues from pay and conditions, levels, progress, curriculum, closing the gap, pupil premium, etc. You can take your pick but it demonstrates you have prepared well and are reading key educational literature."

JAKE CAPPER, TEACHING SCHOOL LEAD, PATHFINDER TEACHING SCHOOL ALLIANCE, YORK

Why should pupils learn your subject?

"Responses to this question should demonstrate enthusiasm for the distinctive nature of a candidate's chosen subject. Transferable skills such as communication or problem-solving skills are fine, but they are not the most important reason for pupils to develop knowledge, skills and understanding in your subject area.

"Evidence of research into recent developments in policy, practice and research in your curriculum area are important here. This is because the mentors who work with student teachers in schools really value the innovations that new entrants to the profession bring. An understanding of pedagogies that can develop a love of your subject is the hallmark of a strong candidate. It's really encouraging to see a candidate who not only knows they want to teach, but also has an embryonic understanding of how they want pupils to experience learning in their classroom."

EMILY SAYERS, SENIOR EDUCATION LECTURER, CANTERBURY CHRIST CHURCH UNIVERSITY

Other common questions

- What do you think makes a good teacher?
- What qualities do you have that will make you a good teacher?
- What are you looking forward to about being a teacher?
- What skills should a teacher have?
- What makes you think you would be a good teacher?
- Why should we take you rather than the other candidates who have applied?
- What skills could you bring to a school?
- How much experience have you had in the classroom?
- What did you learn from your experience?
- What makes a school effective?
- Do you think that the National Curriculum was a good idea? (*If you do not know what the National Curriculum is, look it up!*)
- How would you make sure students had equal opportunities in the classroom?

- What are the differences in teaching in inner London schools?
- What do you think about placing children with Special Educational Needs in mainstream schools?
- What is Every Child Matters? (*If you do not know, look it up!*)
- What would you do if a pupil refused to participate?
- Would you be able to manage/discipline a group of 32 fourteen-year-olds?
- How could you control a class?

You may be asked to complete a numeracy test – particularly in the primary PGCE interviews; this might involve basic mental arithmetic or completing simple maths questions on paper. You may be given a short writing exercise. For instance, one applicant was asked to write a 20-minute essay on 'Are standards in primary schools slipping?' Another had to watch a short film and was then asked how they might use film successfully in teaching.

RECOMMENDED READING

- Dunn, David, *How to be an Outstanding Primary School Teacher*, Continuum Publishing, 2011
- Johnson, Jim, *Passing the Literacy Skills Test (QTS)*, Learning Matters, 2015
- Pattimore, Mark, *Passing the Numeracy Skills Test (QTS)*, Learning Matters, 2015
- Warren, Jessica, *What Makes a Good Teacher*, Createspace Publishing, 2014

Engineering

What is engineering?

There are several different routes into engineering. They include but are not confined to aerospace engineering, civil engineering, electrical and electronic engineering, mechanical engineering and materials engineering.

....

"To be a successful engineer in the present fast-moving technological world you will require an education with the broadest possible interdisciplinary base. As tomorrow's engineer, you will find that your career will involve not only bringing your own specialist knowledge to a project, but also collaborating with engineers from other disciplines and the management of interdisciplinary teams."
UNIVERSITY OF EXETER

This section will focus on civil engineering, although many of the questions are relevant to all branches of engineering. Civil engineering applies science, mathematics, design and creativity to solve problems of critical importance to society across construction, maintenance and management of infrastructure. We tend to take for granted the buildings we live and work in, the roads, railways and airports that allow us to travel, and the water that we use. It is professional civil engineers who make all this possible and who are called on to find solutions to the major challenges facing the world in the future, such as the effects of climate change (including sea level rises), finding sustainable sources of energy and dealing with traffic congestion.

Background to the course

The essential academic skills that admissions tutors look for are numeracy, problem-solving ability and logical thinking. For that reason, you should expect to be asked to do some mental maths as part of the interview. You might also be given a problem to solve that relies on your knowledge of A level Maths and Physics.

Interviewers also look for good communication skills in students, both written and oral. Other positive attributes are IT skills, a practical, hands-on attitude to situations, and design flair and creativity, particularly for courses in civil engineering with architecture. Work experience is useful, so if you mention it in your application, expect to be asked about it.

Most universities do not interview for engineering, but if you apply to Imperial College London, University College London or Oxbridge, do expect an interview.

"As an Admissions Tutor my job is simple: to find out if you would gain the most from studying in our department. Of course, you should have the potential to succeed in a challenging course, as demonstrated by meeting our entry grades, but we're looking beyond your raw marks for a passion in developing your knowledge and understanding of this, the broadest form of engineering."

ADMISSIONS TUTOR, IMPERIAL COLLEGE LONDON

Interview format and outline

At **Imperial College London**, for instance, you will have a 30-minute one-to-one interview with an admissions tutor in their office. This is a conversation rather than a grilling and you should not be overly concerned about it. It will be academic in its focus but the interviewer will also want to find out about you as a person too. This is likely to be the same at other universities. You may be asked to solve a mathematical question.

Sample questions

What part of your physics course have you enjoyed the most (or perhaps found most challenging)?

This is a gentle opener designed to put you at ease by talking about your current A levels. You may also be asked about a project or piece of coursework too, particularly if you mentioned it in your personal statement.

What do you understand by the term 'engineering'?

This is a general starter question and expects you to discuss what engineers do and how the academic study applies to a vocation.

What do you understand by the term 'electrical engineering'?

Clearly, this is asking for specific information about this type of engineering. It is important that you have thought about this in advance. Consider the projects electrical engineers work on, some of the companies they work with and the types of career path they follow.

NOTE: This question would also apply to all the other forms of engineering too.

Give an example of a team-building project you have done.

Engineering is a team business. Think about what times in your recent past you have worked in a team, what role you played and what you learnt.

What are the fundamental differences between engineering and physics?

The interviewer wants to see that you have researched and fully understand your subject. Being able to use examples of the differences between the two disciplines will show that you have at least a basic understanding of the subject.

What considerations would you need to make when designing a bridge?

Scenario questions are becoming increasingly popular with the top universities and they use these broad questions to see how you think. You'll need to walk the interviewer through your thought process and explain why you would make the engineering considerations that you give.

Place a 30cm ruler on top of one finger from each hand so that you have one finger at each end of the ruler, and the ruler is resting on your fingertips. What happens when you bring your fingers together?

In this example almost everyone will expect the ruler to topple off the side where the finger is closest to the centre to the ruler because they expect this finger to reach the centre of the ruler first. They then complete the 'experiment' and find both fingers reach the centre of the ruler at the same time and the ruler remains balanced on two fingers. We like to see how candidates react to what is usually an unexpected result, and then encourage them to repeat the experiment slowly. This helps them observe that the ruler slides over each finger in turn, starting with the finger that is furthest from the centre. With prompting to consider moments and friction, the candidate will conclude that moments mean that there is a larger force on the finger that is closest to the centre of the ruler. This means that there is more friction between the ruler and this finger and therefore the rule slides over the finger furthest from the centre first. This argument will apply until the fingers are the same distance from the centre. The candidate should then be able to explain why both fingers reach the centre of the ruler at the same time, as observed. In some cases, particularly if we have not done a quantitative question already, we might then proceed with a quantitative analysis of forces and moments. We might even discuss

the fact that the coefficient of static friction is higher than the coefficient of dynamic friction and therefore the 'moving' finger gets closer to the centre than the static finger before the finger starts to move over the other finger.
(University of Oxford question and answer)

How would you design a gravity dam for holding back water?

This is a great question because the candidate first should determine the forces acting on the dam before considering the stability of the wall under the action of those forces. Candidates will probably recognise that the water could push the dam over. The candidate would then be expected to construct simple mathematical expressions that predict when this would occur. Some may also discuss failure by sliding, issues of structural design, the effects of water seeping under the dam, and so on. The candidate will not have covered all the material at school so guidance is provided to assess how quickly new ideas are absorbed. The question also probes the candidate's ability to apply physics and maths to new situations and can test interest in and enthusiasm for the engineered world.
(University of Oxford question and answer)

Other common questions

- What are the main differences between the engines in jet fighters and the engines in jet airliners? Which type of engine is the more efficient, and (qualitatively) why?
- What would happen if you drilled through the earth all the way to the other side and then jumped into the hole?
- Why did they used to make mill chimneys so tall?
- If I am in a room with five people and guess all their birthdays, what is the probability of getting (only) one correct?
- Sketch a velocity time graph for a skydiver jumping out of a plane.
- How do you think you could calculate the number of calories that you have burnt after you have gone for a run?
- How does a fridge work?
- What challenges do you think you would be facing as a Formula 1 engineer in 10 years' time?

RECOMMENDED READING

▶ Burnett, James, *Getting into Engineering Courses*, Trotman Education, 2017
▶ Construction News: www.constructionnews.co.uk
▶ www.headstartcourses.org.uk – the website of excellent taster courses in engineering and science. It's well worth looking at.
▶ New Civil Engineer: www.newcivilengineer.com

Medicine and dentistry

What is medicine?

Becoming a doctor isn't an easy option – it takes years of study and hard work. Getting in is just as hard. The standard academic entry criteria are tough and you need to pass a rigorous and testing interview process that is multi-layered. There are many good books on how to succeed as a medical applicant. This section will focus on the core skills and give you the basic facts about what to expect and how to prepare.

If you like helping people there are few more rewarding or respected careers. You'll be part of a team of professionals and non-medical staff delivering care to the highest standards in the NHS. Medicine is about helping people – treating illness, providing advice and reassurance, and seeing the effects of both ill health and good health from the patient's point of view. You need fine interpersonal skills (something that will be tested at interview) as you must work with patients and relatives who are ill or under stress. Being a doctor demands an enquiring mind, the capacity to acquire and maintain high levels of knowledge that must be constantly up to date, and the ability to relate to people as individuals, each with their own health needs.

What is dentistry?

Many of the qualities that are sought after in a potential medic are also highly desirable in a potential dentist. Dentists are clearly interested in the oral health of their clients. It is therefore important that you consider if this rather specific area of healthcare offers what you want in a career. Certainly, if you are interviewed for dentistry, you will be quizzed on this point. You need the same interpersonal skills as those demanded of the medical profession (see above). Where things are different are in two important regards. Firstly, most dentists work alone with the support of a dental nurse. Unlike hospital doctors, they do not work in teams. This is true of course of GPs too, but it is a distinction to think about. Secondly, most dentists are 'generalists' in that they serve the needs of the local community. Some do, of course, work in hospitals. The overwhelming majority, however, are involved in routine dental work.

However, if you like working with your hands, helping people, being creative and being a leader, then you might make a great dentist! This is important as one of the tests that many dentists are asked to take part in when they are interviewed involves manual dexterity. For this reason, it is important to show examples of this dexterity in an application. What does this mean? Well, if you like making clothes, knitting, construction using small parts or have a hobby that requires good hand-eye coordination, these will be worth talking about in your application or interview, if you are shortlisted.

While a career in dentistry may sound appealing, it is important that you are genuinely passionate about oral health – dental school and careers in dentistry are both very demanding, so it will take determination to achieve success in pursuing your dream. The best dentists saw dentistry as their true calling and are constantly working to improve themselves and their abilities.

If you are interested in a career in dentistry, make sure to do some soul searching before plunging head first into the application process. Another great way to figure out if dentistry is right for you is to shadow a dentist or specialist. The experience will allow you to envision yourself doing what he or she does every day. If after this process this still sounds appealing, then dentistry is probably the right fit for you!

Medicine

Please note: While the following information refers to medicine, the dentistry application and interview process follow a very similar format. At the end of the medicine section there is information specifically for dental interviews. However, look at the medical profile too for hints about interview format and questions.

Background to the course

If you have the passion to improve people's lives and the determination to reach the highest standards, you will have many career opportunities. You can follow a path to one of many specialities, from working in a hospital as a surgeon to being based in the community as a GP. The training and support available to you in the NHS can help you to get to the very top of your chosen career.

Medicine is a demanding profession, but one that repays the hard work and dedication it involves through the rich variety of career opportunities it offers. Whether helping patients, managing a hospital or pushing back the frontiers of medical research, you will have the satisfaction of knowing that you are making a positive contribution to society.

At university, you will be kept busy with a mixture of seminars, lectures, anatomy classes, clinical skills practice and patient interaction, depending on where you study. In later years, you will spend more time with medical teams than in the classroom. Assessments may be through exams, written portfolios or practical tests. Medical students are also known for their busy social lives!

Entry standards are high – most universities expect a minimum of three A grade passes at A level (or equivalent), including chemistry. Most medical schools also require you to take the BMAT (www.bmat.org.uk) or UKCAT (www.ukcat.ac.uk). Just as important are a realistic attitude to medical training and clinical practice, a commitment to caring for others, the ability to communicate and work effectively within a team and to appreciate other people's point of view, and a willingness to accept responsibility. The interview will also focus on your work experience and what you learnt from the process, so it is imperative that you reflect on your experience prior to the interview.

Interview format and outline

Both the medical and dentistry interview formats are similar in that they are intense and academic in their emphasis. Many ask you to sit a one-to-one interview and an increasing number will use the MMI format. You may also be asked to complete online questionnaires. The following are insights into the experience of students who attended various schools recently.

University of Exeter Medical School

Interviewers look for evidence that the applicant has the communication skills, reflectiveness and empathy required to become a successful doctor. The interview will be a single panel interview, with two or more interviewers.

"The interview is a structured process of approximately 20 minutes, using a predetermined scoring system. This is to help ensure that candidates receive as close to an identical experience as possible. On each interview day candidates will attend an introductory talk giving further details about the interview process prior to completing pre-interview exercises."
UNIVERSITY OF EXETER MEDICAL SCHOOL

All applicants complete two pre-interview assessments – a written questionnaire that investigates the motivation of the student to study medicine and three ethical scenarios, one of which will be discussed at interview. This process takes about 30 minutes.

King's College London Medical School

King's College uses both panel interviews and the MMI approach. Before the interviews begin, candidates complete a standard questionnaire that examines their understanding of the course, their motivation to study medicine and poses an ethical dilemma to consider.

Multiple Mini Interview (MMI)

An MMI consists of a series of short, structured interview stations used to assess non-cognitive qualities including cultural sensitivity, maturity, teamwork, empathy, reliability and communication skills. Each mini interview involves the candidate being asked a question, which is science based, maths based or ethical. They have two minutes to think about their response before offering their answer. Each station takes about eight to ten minutes to complete and sometimes an actor s used to facilitate a patient/doctor scenario. The duration of the entire interview is usually about two hours.

Generally, the situational questions posed in an MMI touch on the following areas:

- ethical decision making
- critical thinking
- communication skills
- current healthcare and societal issues.

No prior knowledge of medicine is expected. Instead, the interviewers evaluate each candidate's thought process and ability to think on his or her feet.

TOP TIPS FOR MMI SUCCESS

a. Understand the goal of the station – think critically, show integrity, scientific knowledge, empathy and pragmatism. Don't panic, and think before you speak.
b. Work on time management – bring a watch with a digital timer to help your time management. Turn off your mobile phone!
c. Listen to instructions – listen to what you are being asked to do, ask for clarification if you are unsure and listen for cues for information about other stations.

Here are three real MMI questions – many others are available in books. In all three cases, you must speak for eight minutes.

1 A student on your course, a fellow first-year medic, is struggling with his workload. He comes to talk to you and while talking you realise that he may be taking cannabis, a Class B drug. How do you support your friend? Do you have an obligation to inform the university about his drug use?

2 'Liberation Therapy' (LT), a vascular operation developed to potentially cure multiple sclerosis (MS) in certain patients, has recently come under very serious criticism, delaying its widespread use. Among other experimental flaws, critics cite a small sample size in the original evidence used to support LT. As a healthcare policy maker, your job is to weigh the pros and cons in approving novel drugs and therapies. Please discuss the issues you would consider during an approval process for LT.

3   You are walking to this interview and want to be on time. As you pass, you notice that someone has fallen and is bleeding. There is no one around. Should you walk on by, perhaps call 999 on the mobile, but not stop and therefore make the interview on time? Or perhaps you should you stop, call an ambulance, offer first aid and **wait**. This of course, may mean that you miss the interview and fail to win a place at this college. What is the right response?

Norwich Medical School, University of East Anglia (UEA)

This university does something similar to the medical schools at King's College and Exeter. Its interviews last about 50 minutes. They form what is known as an OSCE (Objective Structured Clinical Examination) – the university's term for the MMI. There are seven stations and you spend five minutes at each station. One of the stations is a science question (based on a sound knowledge of biochemistry and not something that should tax an A-grade chemist), another will ask an ethical question and one will be a role play with an actor. You will be asked to explain why you applied to UEA in particular. Make sure that you know why! They ask you directly **'Why should we choose you?'** Expect to be asked about your work experience and the pros and cons of a career in medicine, based on your experience and conversations with young doctors, nurses or other healthcare professionals. Each station has a score of 12. The total score is then turned into a mean average. The good news is that one bad station does not mean you fail.

University of Liverpool School of Medicine

This medical school has a different approach. Its interviews are panel interviews with two academic staff, a local GP or a member of a local NHS Trust. You will be asked about your understanding of the NHS, the role of the doctor as part of the team of medical professionals, how GPs fit into the scenario and your work experience. They are keen to discuss current political issues so a knowledge of the **Liverpool Care Pathway** is advised! Liverpool is also a pioneer of the **problem-based learning** (PBL) approach to medical training. You should be prepared to answer questions about this approach. If you are unfamiliar with this style of teaching, do some research!

Dental interview differences

The **School of Clinical Dentistry at the University of Sheffield** places great store on your awareness of the NHS Constitution and that fact that *'you will need to maintain appropriate levels of professionalism and behaviour in relation to your interactions with colleagues, staff and patients.'*

It recommends that you read and be prepared to answer questions about the standards expected of a dental professional. These are outlined in 'Standards for the Dental Team' and 'Student Fitness to Practise', which can be found on the General Dental Council web page (www.gdc-uk.org).

Interview format and outline

The format will vary, in the same way as the format for medicine varies. I have chosen two schools to compare, but again, check for up-to-date information to ensure that this information remains current.

At the **University of Sheffield**, they interview around 250 applicants a year. They do not use the MMI format that is used by other schools. Interview panels comprise two members of academic staff and a senior dental student. Interviews last up to 15 minutes and investigate:

- career exploration
- values and personal qualities
- commitment to Sheffield
- communication skills.

Communication Station

As part of the interview there will be a Communication Station. This is held separately from the interview. Applicants will have approximately 15 minutes between the end of their interview and the beginning of the Communication Station. Applicants will be presented with a scenario and the station aims to assess:

- communication skills
- empathy
- compassion.

Kings College London Dental Institute offers a very different approach. It follows a process that mirrors that of most medical schools. Applicants will be asked to complete an MMI with up to seven stations. These focus on similar issues to those posed to medics, with an emphasis on ethics, awareness of the demands of the profession and communication skills. Dental MMIs differ from mecical MMIs in that one station tests **manual dexterity**.

There is a very good book about dental MMIs in the recommended reading section (see page 76) – this will help you immensely. The interviewers aren't expecting you to be an expert! Look MMIs and sample questions up online before the interview. You just need a **basic** understanding of **all** the key topics covered in the following sample questions.

Sample questions

Why do you want to do medicine/dentistry?

This is an obvious starting question that needs to be thought about with care. You will need an eloquent and thoughtful answer that shows that you are not doing it for the money, the status, to please your parents or because you think it will be like working at Holby City. Focus on the academic and interpersonal skills you possess, your work experience and your understanding of the role of the NHS in the local community.

What are your plans if you do not succeed first time?

It is a sad but brutal fact that many first-time applicants fail to win a place at medical school. Indeed, for many, the first time is really a glorified dress rehearsal. I know of many former students who failed first time and then got in when they applied the following year. One is a surgeon who failed twice to get into medical school and another is an A&E consultant who read classics and came to medicine in their 20s. So, what will you say if you are asked this question? Would you reapply? Would you take a place on the biomedical science course and then apply as a graduate? Would you walk away and put it down to fate? Whatever you decide, make sure that it is something that you have considered before the interview.

What did you learn from your work experience?

Brighton and Sussex Medical School says clearly that it wants you to discuss what you learnt from the work experience rather than just recounting what you did. The tutor will be looking for evidence that you know what it is like to be a doctor and know a bit about healthcare delivery.

Demonstrate your understanding of scientific and medical issues. Read regularly and widely, particularly in the lead-up to your interview. You ought to be aware of issues in medicine that have been discussed in broadsheet newspapers and scientific journals.

What are the challenges facing the NHS or the medical profession?

Major changes in the field of medicine occur continuously. From a treatments and prescribing perspective, new medicines and techniques appear in journals every week.

There are also diseases which are becoming more common and are starting to threaten the future stability of the NHS. There are many other challenges facing the NHS: the changes to the structure of the NHS are headline news every other week. On a personal level, doctors' pay and pension deals are being adjusted. Be aware of these issues and what is currently in the headlines. Be prepared to talk about aspects such as healthcare rationing, the impact of immigration on waiting lists, access to GPs and nursing homes, or whether we should pay to go to see the GP.

Ethical dilemmas in medicine or dentistry

All medical interviews will include an ethical dilemma. Please note that there is not a right answer to any of these questions. Instead, you must demonstrate the ability to make a reasoned response to an emotive issue and be prepared to engage in a conversation where the interviewer will adopt the contrary position. Expect to be disagreed with, whatever you say!

The following are examples of ethical questions that have been posed to real applicants.

- Is it better to treat a child with cancer than spend the money on care of the elderly? Why?
- Should people who are obese be treated the same as those who are not overweight? If money is scarce should we not discriminate against those who eat too much?
- Should we fund dialysis treatment over a hip replacement?
- Would you preferentially give a liver transplant to someone injured playing rugby as opposed to an alcoholic? Why?
- Do you support euthanasia?
- Should we charge people, based on their means, for treatments they receive on the NHS? If not, should we increase taxation to pay for it?
- Should we force people with cancer to take a course of chemotherapy?
- Should dental treatment be free to all? If so, should we pay more tax to fund it?
- Should parents who fail to care for their children's teeth be prosecuted?

Practise giving answers to all of them (and the many others you will find in books).

Medical ethics is underpinned by the Hippocratic Oath (look it up) and several key principles:

a. informed consent – to consent to a treatment we must have sufficient knowledge to make that decision. If we are not properly informed of the options, are unable to comprehend the options due to ill health or are too young to make such a decision, then this becomes a key issue. It is certainly crucial in the debate on euthanasia – is the person mentally well enough to consent to die?

b. beneficence (acting in a patient's best interests)

c. non-maleficence (not harming the patient)

d. autonomy (respecting the choices of the patient)

e. jurisprudence (assigning resources fairly).

In the question about forcing treatment on a cancer sufferer, the conflict between beneficence and autonomy arises; in the case of dialysis versus hip replacements it is jurisprudence and beneficence. Regarding jurisprudence, it is worth researching something called Quality Adjusted Life Years (QALYs).

To be ahead of the competition in this part of the interview, show you are aware of the above, and be willing to defend your position with wit and intelligence. Don't simply say 'Alcoholics shouldn't have a liver transplant because drinking is bad', as immediately after you will be asked why it is any worse than playing rugby.

Why does your heart rate increase when you exercise?

The simple answer is because you need to deliver more oxygen and nutrients to muscles and remove metabolic products. But follow-up questions would probe whether the student appreciates that there must be a way for the body to know it needs to raise the heart rate, and possible ways for achieving this. Answers might include sensing lowered oxygen or raised carbon dioxide levels. In fact, gas levels might not change much, so students are further asked to propose other signals and ways in which those possibilities could be tested. This probes selection criteria such as problem solving and critical thinking, intellectual curiosity, enthusiasm and curiosity, and the ability to listen.
(Answer from a Univeristy of Oxford admissions tutor)

Why do we have red blood cells?

Initial answers to this question are likely to centre on why the cells are red (the presence of pigmented haemoglobin) and what red cells do (transport oxygen, bound to haemo-globin, from the lungs to cells throughout the body). The real point of this question, however, is to see whether students can offer suggestions as to why haemoglobin is required and why the haemoglobin needs to be contained within red cells and is not free in the plasma. **(Answer from a University of Oxford admissions tutor)**

Other common questions

- What personal qualities do you think are required to become a good doctor?
- What was your favourite part of chemistry A level? Why?
- How good are you at mental arithmetic? Why is this important for a doctor?
- How do you cope with stress?
- What is the role of the General Medical Council (GMC)?
- What do you know about the career progression of doctors in the UK?
- What can you tell me about the structure of the Modernising Medical Careers (MMC) training programme?
- Tell us about the role of the National Institute for Health and Care Excellence (NICE).
- Give us an example of a time when you worked as part of a team.
- What have you learnt about your strengths and weaknesses from your work experience/voluntary work?
- Describe three problems with the NHS.
- What are your thoughts on the lack of NHS staffing levels in the UK, and how might the government address this?
- How do you think the government should tackle the UK's growing obesity levels?
- The UK's population is ageing. What does this mean for the future of the NHS?
- Will Brexit affect the NHS?

Other common *dental only* questions

- You might be asked about fundamental dental conditions such as **caries, tooth erosion, dentine hypersensitivity** or **gum disease**.
- You could be asked what you understand by the terms **endodontics, periodontics** or **oral surgery**.
- You may be asked about the **dental amalgam debate** – this is the contentious issue of the use of mercury in fillings. Another common question asked relates to **water fluoridisation**.

RECOMMENDED READING

- Barton, James and Horner, Simon, *Getting into Medical School 2018 Entry*, Trotman Education, 2017
- Coli, Mariam, *Multiple Mini Interviews (MMI) for UK Dental School*, Fast Track Dentistry, 2014
- Cross, Adam, *Getting into Dental School*, Trotman Education, 2017
- Griffiths, Dr Peter, *Ace Your Medical School Interview: Includes Multiple Mini Interviews MMI for Medical School*, CreateSpace Independent Publishing Platform, 2013
- Becoming a Doctor, BMA website: www.bma.org.uk
- General Medical Council: www.gmc-uk.org
- Tomorrow's Doctors, GMC website: www.gmc-uk.org/Tomorrow_s_Doctors_1214.pdf_48905759.pdf
- Want to be a Doctor: www.wanttobeadoctor.co.uk – a fantastic website that provides great advice about applications to this competitive course.

Nursing and midwifery

What is nursing?

Nursing is a unique occupation and offers you a chance to help others when they need it most. There has never been a more exciting time to join the profession. Nurses are crucial members of the multi-professional healthcare team. Furthermore, the number and variety of nursing roles are extensive. Once qualified as a registered nurse you will have opportunities to work in a range of environments including NHS and independent hospitals, GP surgeries, clinics, nursing and residential homes, occupational health services, voluntary organisations, the armed forces and industry. Today there are greater opportunities for nurses to take increased responsibility for patient care and to become specialists and advanced practitioners in many areas; for example, intensive care, cancer care and mental health.

What is midwifery?

Midwives offer individual care to women and their families and help them take part in their own care planning during pregnancy. Both during and after pregnancy you will be with the new mother in her own locality. Midwifery is as much about supporting the new mother and her partner as about helping with the birth of the baby. Support continues from the confirmation of the pregnancy through to the postnatal days after the baby is born.

All potential nurses and midwives are interviewed as part of the selection process. This is primarily to see if they have the interpersonal qualities needed for this hands-on profession. Many patients are vulnerable and pregnant women need specialist care. As a result, expect plenty of questions that will focus on soft skills, listening, coping with stress and managing patients from all backgrounds and cultures. Expect to be asked about the current nature of the profession, changes in nursing practice and the role of the midwife in the whole of obstetrics. It is compulsory for all people wanting to qualify as a nurse or midwife to complete a degree first. You will also be asked to undergo a Disclosure and Barring Service (DBS) check and healthcare screening as part of the application process. This is undertaken after you are offered a place and before you enrol. It is not part of the interview process.

Background to the courses

Nurses and midwives play a crucial role in the NHS, providing care to patients both in hospital (inpatients) and visiting the hospital for treatment or care (outpatients). They also have a community role and may visit people in their homes to offer care, advice and support. Both courses are vocational and this means that you will train to become a practitioner in the same way as dentistry courses or veterinary courses train future dentists or vets.

Teaching will be in lectures but a lot of the learning takes place in situ on wards. You will meet and treat patients, with supervision, from the first year onwards, so when you are interviewed the selectors will want to see how your interpersonal skills will cope with this demanding role. Manual dexterity and basic numeracy are important and will be assessed too. It is vital of course that you can assess appropriate doses and have the confidence to inject patients or intubate them.

BSc courses tend to last for three years and all courses are accredited by the Nursing and Midwifery Council to ensure that the teaching and content meet all the minimum standards. Once qualified you will be licensed to practise in the UK. If you are an overseas applicant, then you may well be asked to take an IELTS (International English Language Testing System) language assessment at the time of application.

Interview format and outline

Unlike medicine, the standard format for a nursing and midwifery place will be a panel interview. That being said, recently, highly compettive nursing courses (such as that at King's College London) are starting to use the MMI. This particularly true of universities that offer both medicine and nursing courses. For more details on this, see pages 68–70.

At **King's College London** (whose nursing and midwifery courses are among the most prestigious) all applicants complete a literacy and numeracy test before the interview begins. This is to ensure that you have a sound understanding of written English and adequate numeracy skills to cope with dosages and using charts.

The King's College numeracy test *'comprises 15 questions and is designed to assess your overall numerical skills. Basic calculators are provided on the day. We strongly suggest that you use this sample numeracy test to prepare for the test and you can access external numeracy revision resources at https://snap-services.org, and we strongly suggest that you register and use this to prepare for the test.'*

The King's College literacy test *'will be used to assess general literacy skills and will involve you analysing a set text. The skills being assessed include identifying the main points of a text and differentiating them from subsidiary points; recognising implied meaning; scanning for specific information; identifying the writer's opinion, attitude and purpose; following the line of an argument; grammar, spelling and punctuation.'*

You can download sample tests for both that you ought to practise. In reality, if you have a good pass in Maths and English GCSE, you will be just fine!

King's College's MMI advice is varied but essentially it is as follows.

- Make sure that you understand the NHS Core Values.
- The MMI will last about 30 minutes and will include video clips of patients discussing their experience that you will be asked to comment on.
- You should think about some of the ethical issues that surround nursing and midwifery – including the challenging topics of abortion and surrogacy.

There will often be a short one-to-one interview where your UCAS personal statement will be discussed. The MMI will be led by interviewers who may include academics, current students, an NHS Trust representative and members of the general public who have been trained to provide a layperson's insight.

Role play is often a method used in nursing interviews. One student I know recalled having to interview *'a man who'd had cancer of the larynx which required removal. What did that mean? He couldn't speak! Ever had an interview with someone who couldn't speak? That was a real challenge given the four minutes I had were ticking by. He said some students treated him like he had a mental disability. Others treated him like he was deaf. Others couldn't understand him at all, panicked that he was an actual cancer patient and just froze.'*

If you have dyslexia or another learning need, you should always let the university know in advance so that they can give you extra time.

Sample questions

Why do you want to become a nurse or midwife?
Make sure that you are aware of the current issues facing entrants to the profession.

"Be clear about why you want to be a nurse – why you have chosen this field of nursing; what do you know about the role and responsibilities of a nurse in this area; are you familiar with current evidence base. Good websites to look at are the Nursing and Midwifery Council, Royal College of Nursing, Royal College of Midwifery and the Nursing Times. Be ready to answer questions about the profession – brief yourself on current issues such as the Francis Report and other news stories. Think about how your life experiences are relevant in preparing you for midwifery or get practical experience in a volunteer capacity if you can. Show your enthusiasm and commitment."

UNIVERSITY OF SOUTH WALES

What do you understand by the term 'professional'? What qualities do you need?

This is an important question as it is used to gauge your integrity and moral compass. You are being asked to consider what you think are the key skills of a good professional – these might include honesty, patience and diligence. You are going to be a licensed professional nurse or midwife and the reputation of the hospital and the profession will be judged, in part, by your actions. For this reason, it is important that you present yourself as a serious person who understands the importance of the position and its responsibility. You need to show that you have a good sense of right and wrong.

What do you know of the roles and responsibilities of a midwife?

This question assesses your awareness of the reality of the profession and how this differs from its portrayal in the media. This is where your work experience and meetings with practitioners will help. Try to answer this question in such a way as to expose your understanding and perception of a career in midwifery or nursing.

Other common MMI questions

- If a patient asked you – a student nurse – to increase their pain relief as they are in agony, but you know that they have already had their full dosage, what would you do?
- If a fellow student was suffering from stress and disclosed that they took cannabis to help them relax, would you inform the university?
- Give an example of what you learnt from a work experience placement that helped you decide to apply.
- How do you manage stress and timekeeping?

Other common questions

- What do you think the public expect from a midwife?
- What current issues in midwifery are of concern to you?
- What do you know about the NMC and registration?
- What can you tell me about the Nursing Code of Practice?
- Where does nursing take place?
- How do you deal with criticism and/or authority?
- What do you know about current nursing issues in the media?
- What challenges affect nursing in the UK?
- How would you cope with the death of a patient?
- What does confidentiality mean and why is it important?
- What do you know about consent?

RECOMMENDED READING

- The Nursing and Midwifery Council: www.nmc.org.uk
- Royal College of Nursing: www.rcn.org.uk

TOP TIP

When answering an interview question, you should try
to respond with enough detail so that you meet the
admissions criteria and try to include a 'real life' example.

© The University of Manchester

Occupational therapy and radiotherapy

What are occupational therapy and radiotherapy?

Occupational therapy and radiotherapy are both professions that are allied to medicine. They are very different roles within the NHS but I have put them together for the purposes of this book because universities normally include an interview as part of the applicant assessment process.

What is occupational therapy?

Occupational therapy is a science degree-based health and social care profession, regulated by the Health and Care Professions Council (HCPC). Most degree courses are three years in length and lead to a BSc. Occupational therapy takes a holistic approach to patient care, looking after patients' mental and physical health. Occupational therapists work alongside other health professions, often physiotherapists, to help someone who is recovering from ill health or injury to cope with day-to-day living.

This helps to increase the patient's independence and satisfaction in all aspects of life.

'Occupation' refers to practical and purposeful activities that allow people to live independently and have a sense of identity. This could be essential daily tasks such as self-care, work or leisure. Occupational therapists work with adults and children of all ages with a wide range of conditions, most commonly those who have difficulties due to a mental health conditions, physical or learning disabilities. They can work in a variety of settings including health organisations, social care services, housing, education, prisons, voluntary organisations or as independent practitioners.

What is radiotherapy?

Radiotherapists work alongside oncologists, and other professions too, to treat cancer and other diseases by administering radiation treatment. They are also trained in the use of equipment that uses radiation, so they might operate X-ray machines, administer radiation drugs and monitor the patient's welfare while they are undergoing treatment. Most radiotherapists complete the three-year degree programme or take the two-year postgraduate PgD or MSc course. There are two routes and it is important to consider which one suits you best. One is diagnostic and the other therapeutic. The diagnostic route specialises in interpreting data and making decisions about the care of the patient. The therapeutic route specialises in administering treatment plans. Both routes are covered to some extent in most courses, but take care to look at the course outline before you apply.

Background to the courses

Occupational therapy and radiotherapy courses are vocational, which means that your learning will be split between traditional lectures and on-the-job training alongside current practitioners. All the courses will be accredited by the HCPC and you will be working towards admission into either the Royal College of Occupational Therapists or the Society and College of Radiographers. As you will be asked to take a hands-on role from the first year onwards, the selection process will assess your interpersonal (people) skills to ensure that you have the aptitude to work in a patient environment.

Interview format and outline

The two disciplines have a very similar selection process, so the information here will combine questions and suggestions from leading providers of both courses. As with everything though, this is a guide and a starting point. You must be proactive and look carefully at the websites of the universities that offer the course to establish which one suits you best.

Occupational therapy

The admissions route for occupational therapy courses is similar to that of radiotherapy courses.

The **University of Southampton** places a great deal of weight on your personal statement and scores an applicant accordingly. If the score is high enough and the academic predictions are sound, then the candidate will be invited to interview. Southampton looks for evidence in the personal statement that you have answered the following questions.

- **Why do you want to be an occupational therapist?** What is it about your attitudes, values and character that makes this profession so appropriate for you?
- **What do you understand about the role?** To further strengthen your application, it is important that you demonstrate a clear insight into your chosen profession and the scope of the role. This should hopefully be achieved by reflecting on relevant work experience, volunteering or shadowing that you may have undertaken.
- **Discuss your relevant academic preparation.** What have you particularly enjoyed during your studies and how do you feel this has prepared you for this degree? Discuss any particularly relevant projects/coursework you may have undertaken.
- **Personal interests.** Sports/music/drama/volunteering/job/responsibilities/relaxing/ etc. Identify transferable skills that will be useful in your chosen profession.

If you are called to interview, then you will be asked about the personal statement as part of a short panel interview.

Southampton has a selection day, which involves a tour, panel interview and some online tests. You will also be asked to complete a written test, in which you must respond to some information that you are given. This does not presume any specific knowledge of the profession. You are normally given 60 minutes to complete this task. Finally, there is a large group discussion where you are given the chance to ask questions and discuss the role of the occupational therapist. The discussion is used to assess your communication skills, so ASK QUESTIONS and respond to questions.

The **University of Brighton** has a similar structure to its selection, but does not require you to complete online tests. It uses group interviews to assess your ability.

Brighton also requires you to complete two 500-word reports on the role of two different occupational therapy services. Applicants who work in an occupational therapy service can use this for one of the reports. The two services should be in different areas, ideally a mental health and a physical setting. The reports should be attached to the personal statement section on the online application. Events are organised by the School of Health Sciences to assist applicants with writing their reports and the events involve attendance at two teaching sessions. Details of these events can be found online.

This is a different and quite significant requirement and shows how important it is to research and fully understand the demands of each school before applying.

Both Southampton and Brighton will need to see evidence of work experience and will want you to discuss this in the application and interview. All healthcare courses have the same standards regarding DBS and health clearances.

"Universities like you to have shadowed two OTs [occupational therapists] in different settings (preferably one physical and one mental health). Don't feel shy arranging this, it's a common requirement for entry onto health courses such as OT, physiotherapy and nursing. So common is it that some hospitals have shadowing days where a number of prospective students get to talk to different OT departments. Where do you start? When I was deciding on my career change I telephoned the HR/personnel department of my local hospital to ask if I could shadow and observed three departments, audiology, speech and language therapy, and orthoptics, and no one batted an eyelid. I would certainly recommend doing it as it was one of the most useful things that I did to help me make a career change."

ADMISSIONS TUTOR, UNIVERSITY OF SALFORD

Sample questions

Why do you want to become an occupational therapist?

This is an obvious opening question. Make sure that you understand the role of the occupational therapist alongside the other medical professions. Draw on any work experience or conversations you have had with professionals. Show an awareness of the need to work with people of all backgrounds and ages. Ensure that you discuss any work you may have done with the elderly, as these are often people you will treat, and who may be recovering from strokes or ill health.

Why did you apply to this university?

Think about your reasons for choosing this course. They may well be straightforward: it is near home or some friends have recommended it. They may be more complex: the university may have an excellent teaching reputation, or employment record, or offer good support for people with disabilities or have access to hardship funds.

What personal qualities and key skills do you think you need to become a good occupational therapist?

The key points to emphasise are your excellent communication skills (provide evidence), your empathy, resilience, patience, calm persona and willingness to work with people of all ages. You must be able to communicate with people who are ill or sometimes scared. You may, if working with children, have to show an ability to make complex ideas straightforward. You will also have to deal with sometimes hostile relatives. You will need a degree of physical strength and to be organised so as to manage your workload efficiently. Finally, and perhaps most importantly, you need to be a good listener!

Other common questions

- How do you think an occupational therapist works with other healthcare professionals?
- Describe what you think an occupational therapist's role involves.
- What do you think are the most important skills that are required to become an occupational therapist?
- Do you possess these skills? If so, can you give examples to demonstrate this?

Radiotherapy

"The interview was classed as informal but most people were dressed semi-smart (trousers and a shirt/top). Otherwise the interview was relatively relaxed. Do be prepared for the usual type of questions: 'Why this course?', 'Will you be able to cope with the placement/academic workload?'. And have a couple of questions of your own. There was also some very nice cake at the end!"

FIRST YEAR RADIOTHERAPY STUDENT, UNIVERSITY OF BRIGHTON

The University of West of England (UWE) offers the BSc in Radiotherapy and Oncology and has a similar selection process.

The admissions tutors will read the UCAS application and expect to see that a candidate meets the minimum academic entry standards. This will include GCSE and A level (or equivalent) grades. The UWE entry criteria are likely to be different from similar courses, so check the appropriate literature and/or the online prospectus. DO check carefully to see which course has an entry profile that best suits yours. If English is not your first language you will need to have obtained a 6.5 in the IELTS language test.

All applicants will be assessed to see if they conform with Health Care England's Value Based Recruitment Framework, which is available to read online. It is very important that you do read it before applying. If you succeed at interview, and accept an offer, you will be subject to a health assessment and vaccinations. It is important that you are in good health and have the capacity to work in a hospital environment. You will need to liaise with your GP to prove that you have had certain inoculations. You will also have a Disclosure Barring Service (DBS) check to ensure that you are fit to work with children and vulnerable adults.

The radiotherapy selection day at UWE will include a 30-minute written task related to the skills and attributes that are required for the profession. You will also have a panel interview that will last 15 minutes. This will be conducted by an academic and a practising radiotherapist. At this interview you will be expected to talk about your work experience. Indeed, it is a formal requirement for most courses that you undertake a **minimum** of one full day's work experience where you shadow a therapeutic radiotherapist. If you secure more than one placement, or if you can talk about meetings you have had with radiotherapists or with patients who have undergone radiotherapy, then this will aid your application. You will be expected to complete a Clinical Visits Report Form (available online) to explain where you went and what you learnt from the experience.

Cardiff University has a very similar structure to its selection process, with the exception that it scores the personal statement according to certain criteria and this helps in choosing who to interview. The university states that *'applicants will need to demonstrate that they possess the personal attributes and qualities required of a therapeutic radiographer to be able to provide the necessary care and support for cancer service users. This will be achieved through the personal statement which will be scored according to the following predetermined criteria for shortlisting:*

- *a knowledge of and commitment to the profession of therapeutic radiography*
- *a caring attitude towards people*
- *a willingness to accept responsibility*
- *evidence of working as part of a team*
- *evidence of a broad spectrum of interests and personal achievements.'*

If you are shortlisted, you will be invited to an interview that will follow the MMI format used for medicine, dentistry and some other courses. Clearly, the questions will be subtly different but the overall pattern will be the same. For details, look at the profiles on medicine and dentistry in this book.

You will visit six MMI stations and you will be assessed at each for about five minutes. Cardiff is at pains to say that there are no right and wrong answers. These stations do not expect any knowledge of radiotherapy and are designed to see if the candidate can *'think on their feet, appraise information, communicate information and ideas and demonstrate that they have thought about some of the issues relevant to the profession of therapeutic radiography'.*

Sample questions

Why do you want to study radiotherapy?
This is an obvious question to be asked that will assess your understanding of the course and the nature of the profession. Make sure that you understand the difference between therapeutic and diagnostic radiotherapy and that you can discuss what you learnt while on your work experience placement.

What personal qualities do you have that make you suitable for a career as a radiotherapist?

Again, this is an obvious question that tests how perceptive you are. Ensure that you mention your listening skills and your ability to put people at ease. You will work with people of all ages, so perhaps talk about how you enjoy meeting people from all backgrounds. You will also need to be calm, to have good time management skills and to be able to explain or interpret data.

Other common questions

- Why did you apply to this university?
- Talk to me about what you did on the work placement and explain how it helped you to decide that this was the course for you.
- What are your plans after you've graduated? Do you aim to work in the NHS, or pursue other opportunities at private clinics and industry?
- What aspects of a radiotherapy role appeal to you most?
- How do you think radiotherapy is beneficial to others?
- What are your plans after you've completed your degree?
- Why are you applying for diagnostic radiography, and not therapeutic? (*Clearly this is a question that can be reversed!*)
- What do you think will be the most challenging aspect of your degree?
- What is a sonographer?

RECOMMENDED READING

- McKenna, Chris, *Becoming An Occupational Therapist: Is Occupational Therapy Really the Career for You?* BPP Learning Media, 2012
- NHS Careers website: www.healthcareers.nhs.uk

Performing and creative arts – drama, music and art

What are the performing and creative arts?

Performing arts is a catch-all phrase for any arts subject that includes an element of performance. This would include courses that involve the teaching of acting, music and dance. This profile will cover a range of these, but it is not designed to be a comprehensive review of all of them. The creative arts are normally those that involve art and design as part of the brief. To this end, I will focus on the Foundation art course, which is a prerequisite for most fine art degrees in the UK.

The interview process for these courses differs from many others in that it will often involve an audition, where the applicant is asked to play an instrument, perform an extract from a play, dance a piece that they have devised or sing. Applicants will probably be interviewed as well, but the interview is often secondary to the audition in the selection process. Foundation art courses normally interview on a one-to-one basis, but they will use the portfolio of work provided by the applicant as a means to draw out the applicant's passion for art and their suitability for a place on a course. Sometimes interviews are conducted on Skype, and often the candidate will need to upload photos of their work in advance. One college in London asks for the portfolio to be delivered on a specific day and then collected at the end of the day. This is not the same day as the interview and an interview is offered only if the portfolio is deemed acceptable.

Background to the courses

The courses are diverse and what follows is a summary of the primary elements of each. Unlike for most other courses, the interviews will be largely performative. So questions that you may be asked will focus on your audition pieces, the influences you have had – and, in the case of art, your portfolio.

As with all the other subject profiles in this book, this is a taster and it is very important that you do your own research to ensure you understand the demands of each college or school.

Acting

The first thing to say is that acting courses are not the same as many university drama courses. Many university courses combine drama with English or another subject. Drama in these courses tends to focus on the study of plays, in the way that perhaps A level Theatre

Studies focuses on the history of drama and certain playwrights. That is not always the case, of course, and some university and college courses are very performance based.

Please take care though to look carefully at the profiles of both the acting and drama courses on the UCAS website to ensure they are what you want.

This profile will focus on the courses that simply offer a formal vocational training in acting, designed to prepare you for a career as an actor. A recent survey on the website https:// actinginlondon.co.uk suggested that the top 10 drama schools in the UK are:

- Guildford School of Acting
- London Academy of Music and Dramatic Art (LAMDA)
- Manchester School of Theatre at Manchester Metropolitan University
- Mountview Academy of Theatre Arts
- Rose Bruford College of Theatre and Performance
- Royal Academy of Dramatic Art (RADA)
- Royal Central School of Speech and Drama
- Royal Conservatoire of Scotland
- Royal Welsh College of Music and Drama
- Sylvia Young Theatre School.

This profile will focus on three drama schools to show how they differ and compare. I have **not chosen these in rank order,** and every school named above and many others not mentioned in the list have great merit. Once again – do your research and make an informed choice. There is no such thing as the best school, there only is the best school for YOU! Rather than using interviews in their selection process, most drama schools require applicants to attend an audition, both as part of a group and individually. Most demand a fee to cover the cost of the audition. This can vary but seems to average at £40.

Guildford School of Acting – University of Surrey

"I really felt like GSA wanted to prepare me as much possible for the industry. Everything seemed to walk hand in hand with each other; what I learnt in one group singing class I could easily apply to my Shakespearean methodology."

STUDENT AT GUILDFORD SCHOOL OF ACTING, UNIVERSITY OF SURREY

As with many schools of acting, Guildford offers a range of courses to suit your talents. These include BAs in dance, musical theatre, acting and actor musician.

The acting course is intense and the teaching draws on the practices of Stanislavsky and Lecog, as well as Sanford Meisner and Mike Alfreds. If these are names you are unfamiliar with, do some research before you apply so that you can speak about them with a degree of confidence in the application and interview. Guildford teaches through improvisation and the use of scripts, and you will also learn about screen acting alongside theatre, to prepare you well for professional auditions.

If you meet the minimum academic standards, which are high, you will be selected for an interview.

Guildford asks all applicants to prepare two audition pieces – one pre-1800 and the other post-1800. They should be monologues that last no more than two minutes. They should be in your own accent and be appropriate for an actor of your age. You may be asked to perform these pieces more than once and you may be asked to reinterpret the piece imagining that you are older, younger or someone from a different part of the UK. In addition, you should expect to take part in a theatre workshop with other applicants, where improvisation and theatre games will be part of the assessment.

Many applicants will be called back for a second audition, so do not be surprised if you are. You are asked to be flexible about this. Acting applicants are not interviewed one to one.

Music and dance courses

Clearly, if you apply for a course with a music or dance component, you will be asked to audition using these skills too. The singing audition will require you to prepare two songs to demonstrate your vocal range. One should be a musical theatre piece. There may also be a group singing audition. Musicians will be asked to play a piece on their chosen instrument. For dance auditions, you will not be asked to prepare formal audition pieces. Instead, you will be graded according to your performance in dance workshops. You will be interviewed and the questions will include the following.

- What is your background in dance?
- What form of dance classes have you attended?
- Did you take grades?
- What performance work have you done? Can you describe the work and how you prepared for it?
- Which choreographer would you love to work with and why?

- What is your opinion on contemporary dance as opposed to classical dance?
- What are your career aspirations?

Musicians will also have a short one-to-one interview which will focus on their musicianship, vocal versatility, agility and optimum vocal health.

Manchester School of Theatre, Manchester Metropolitan University

The School offers the BA Acting course and the application process is similar to that of Guildford, in that you apply through UCAS. The academic entry requirements are lower than for Guildford, due in part to the academic profile of the university.

Applicants are auditioned. You will be expected to prepare three pieces, one from Shakespeare (in blank verse), one from a play written post-1970 and a third piece from any source you like. There will also be a group workshop and you are asked to wear comfortable, loose clothing.

The School offers some very good generic advice about what it is looking for, as well as guidance on choosing an audition piece and preparing for the audition. What follows is a summation of its advice, together with some tips from other schools too.

Choosing a piece and delivering it well

- Choose your pieces well in advance and choose them to suit your skill level. The audition panel is looking for potential, not the finished product.
- Choose pieces that are short and engaging. There are many good books with suggestions for pieces. One good book recommended by several colleges is *The Excellent Audition Guide* by Andy Johnson, published by Nick Hern Books.
- Do not deliver the piece directly to the audition panel. If your character is speaking to the audience, then place the audience just behind and above the panel.
- Choose a piece that you find exciting – don't pick something that you think the panel will like. Pick something that speaks to you and that you can be fully engaged in too.
- Choose pieces that are ACTIVE; pieces in which the character wants something, now, from someone else. The 'someone else' might be a character in the play or could be the audience. Avoid story pieces in which the character is recalling a previous event.
- Pick a piece that is unusual – in that sense, read around a bit and avoid the obvious – 'To be or not to be …'

- Remember to engage your body in the work – acting is vocal *and* physical.
- Arrive on time and give yourself time to relax and calm down before you perform.

What the audition panel is looking for

- Someone who listens and responds well to others in the group workshops.
- People who take some risks – they choose unusual pieces or have a strong physical presence.
- Someone who owns and personalises dramatic language.
- A credible and appropriate investigation of character and situation.
- Someone who can show a clear contrast between the chosen speeches.
- Effective and sensitive use of voice and physicality in the chosen speeches and the practical workshop.
- An applicant who demonstrates spatial awareness and sensitivity to their environment and works co-operatively with others.
- Someone with energy and confidence.
- Someone with the concentration and focus that is needed for ALL the tasks.

Royal Conservatoire of Scotland

The application process here is very similar, but as this is a conservatoire you will have a different range of students on campus. The Conservatoire has a very similar format to its competitors for interviews in acting, and suggests that for the audition you prepare two speeches to perform in character. One should be from a play by William Shakespeare, preferably in verse, and the other a contrasting contemporary piece of your own choice. I pick the Conservatoire as a place to look at for two reasons. Firstly, its website has a very good online video on preparing for auditions, presented by Ali de Souza, a lecturer at the Conservatoire. Secondly, this is a place where ALL the performing arts come together, which will greatly enrich your higher education experience.

After the initial audition, a decision is made in the afternoon to recall certain applicants. If you are selected, you will be put into a group workshop for further assessment. You will also be asked to perform at least one of your pieces again before the recall panel. The panel will then work with you on one of your pieces and you will be given a sight-reading test.

Unusually, you will then be asked to attend a short panel interview. Here you will be asked a few questions, and you are urged to be honest in your answers.

Sample questions

Why do you want to be an actor/actress?

Try not to be obvious in your answer – 'I always wanted to act since I was a child.' That may well be the case, but try to think of an answer that is different. For instance, your interest in acting might have been sparked by a performance in a play, a visit to the theatre, a chance encounter with an actor, attendance at a summer school, etc.

Which actor(s) do you admire?

Avoid the obvious big names – we all know about the A-list Hollywood stars. What about thinking about an actor with a less well-known profile but a strong CV? You might want to mention someone with a well-known theatre profile rather than a TV presence. Or you could talk about someone such as David Tennant, who has a profile that covers both.

How do you feel about the performance you gave in your audition?

Don't put yourself down, but don't try to make out that you're the greatest actor that ever lived. Constructive criticism of your performance and evaluating your strengths and weaknesses shows the interviewer that you know what you need to do to improve your performance in the future.

What are your career aspirations?

Be honest but PRAGMATIC. Don't appear starry-eyed about the harsh reality of making a career in acting. Show some awareness and be self-effacing.

What did you think of the last play/performance you saw?

This could be anything from a serious dramatic performance to the Christmas pantomime. Talk about the style of play, the acting, script, lighting and any other aspects of the performance that stood out to you. If you've seen similar plays or plays by the same writer/director/producer, then you could also use these for comparison.

Why did you choose this school?

Clearly, this could be a loaded question, as it presumes that you are aware of the school's history, profile, alumni and reputation in the business. Make sure that before you attend the audition you VISIT the school informally, read the literature, and perhaps even chat informally to a student. That sort of dedication will not be ignored.

The music conservatoire

Most conservatoires offer music, but many also offer courses in drama and other performing arts. The emphasis here is on performance. Unlike degree courses, the academic element is reduced and the applicant will be expected to show a high level of performance potential, normally via audition.

You can apply only once in a cycle and the process is not that dissimilar to the process followed by other undergraduate applicants.

Note: Not all UK conservatoires use the UCAS process. Some have their own application form. Currently the Guildhall School of Music and Drama (www.gsmd.ac.uk) does not use the UCAS Conservatoires system and has its own application form and audition process. Please contact this school direct to obtain the latest prospectus or complete the online application form.

Here is the current list of institutions that use the UCAS Conservatoires scheme:

- Birmingham Conservatoire
- Leeds College of Music
- Royal Academy of Music
- Royal College of Music
- Royal Conservatoire of Scotland
- Royal Northern College of Music
- Royal Welsh College of Music
- Trinity Laban College of Music and Drama.

It is important to note that the UCAS Conservatoires system is used for applications to institutions that offer a full range of courses, which may include music, drama, dance or musical theatre. Conservatoires are not exclusively for outstanding performance musicians. The next few paragraphs will provide you with a sound understanding of why students apply to a conservatoire and what to expect at audition.

Why study at a conservatoire?

A conservatoire education is suitable for any talented musician who is particularly interested in performance, conducting or composition. They teach to a professional standard, combining practical and academic study in an environment that is steeped in musical history. Many of the teachers are leaders in their field and the UK is fortunate to have some of the finest conservatoires in Europe. Studying in a conservatoire environment enables excellent networking and developmental opportunities for all musicians, regardless of their specialism or musical direction. As the Royal Conservatoire of Scotland points out, *'The curriculum is centred around performance – it's what we do.'*

Conservatoire students have the opportunity to conduct, perform or have their music performed on numerous occasions. Many of the performances are public and the students often find it is possible to earn money while at college by playing at private events and other functions. The range of music teaching available is vast, including jazz, orchestral, operatic, musical theatre and choral.

As you can imagine, competition for places is high. Your traditional academic standards play second fiddle to your performance standard. Each conservatoire has its own academic and performance demands. However, I will use information provided by the Royal College of Music (RCM) and the Royal Conservatoire of Scotland (RCS) to provide you with an idea of the demands likely to be placed on you and any other applicant. Most of this information is relevant to all applicants but you are advised to look carefully at the prospectuses of each of the conservatoires.

Audition format and outline

The **Royal College of Music** (RCM) has the following audition format.

Auditions/interviews are approximately 15–20 minutes long. For some instruments and for voice you may be asked to perform at a second audition on the same day. For set pieces, see the Audition Pieces section of the online prospectus.

Sight-reading may be required of all performers. An accompanist can be provided by the RCM if required, but you are strongly advised to bring your own accompanist, with whom you will have worked in preparation for the audition.

Please note, each institution has its own audition procedure. Please research this information carefully before proceeding.

At the **Royal Conservatoire of Scotland** (RCS), a strong indication of potential is sought at the entrance audition for this programme. Successful applicants will normally be of a standard at least equivalent to Grade 8 with Distinction of the Associated Board of the Royal Schools of Music in their principal instrument. The RCS points out that the audition is designed to be fair and two-way. It is a chance for you to assess if the RCS is the right fit for you and vice versa. They assess you based on several key criteria including the audition, your commitment to the programme as shown by the personal statement and interview, your practical experience, academic profile and references.

The audition will be in the applicant's principal instrument, including voice. An accompanist will be provided where applicable, but an applicant can bring their own with advanced permission. All applicants get sufficient time to practise with the accompanist prior to the audition. In addition, all applicants get 10 minutes' warm-up time immediately prior to the audition.

The audition piece should not exceed 10 minutes in length and it is common for the audition to be paused early if the panel has reached a consensus on the performance. This is not a bad sign!

The RCS provides clear guidance online about what instrumentalists should expect in all major instruments, including the audition piece choice and the scale and sight-reading expected. It is clearly vital that you check this information carefully in advance.

Interviews are not required unless you apply for the Music Composition course. Here you will be asked to comment on two submitted compositions, which will include recordings of the pieces. The entrance audition *'will consist of an interview in which applicants will be encouraged to demonstrate a detailed knowledge of varied repertoire. Applicants will be asked about how they began composing or how they were introduced to composition; and they will be invited to talk about the compositions they have submitted. Applicants will also be asked about their aspirations as a composer. Successful candidates will show style, imagination, an adventurous approach to composition and above all, potential to develop their beliefs and skills through the programme.'*

Art Foundation

Most people who aspire to read fine art or design at degree level will be asked to complete an art Foundation course. Art Foundation courses are taught over one year and are intense and teacher-led within a professional studio environment. They tend to focus on four key areas:

- visual communication – graphic design, advertising, packaging, bookbinding, art direction, film, illustration, moving image and model making
- three-dimensional design – architecture, landscape architecture, interior, product, furniture, prop and set design

- fashion and fabrication – menswear, womenswear, costume, fashion journalism and constructed textiles
- fine art – painting, mixed media, printmaking, installation, sculpture, performance and photography.

Most applicants have an A level or equivalent in art or design plus a pass at Grade C/4 in GCSE English and Maths. There is an unofficial ranking of art Foundation colleges, but so much depends on fashion, and some colleges rise or fall in popularity, for reasons that are hard to pinpoint.

The other key issue is funding. Although art Foundation courses are funded, there are no grants or loans for living expenses. As a result, many applicants live at home and their choice of foundation course is limited by geography. Most applications are made directly to the college via online application forms, and not through UCAS.

Below are some of the most popular institutions for the art Foundation course:

- Arts University Bournemouth
- Central Saint Martins
- Chelsea College of Arts
- Kingston University
- Loughborough University
- Oxford Brookes University
- Sheffield Hallam University
- Plymouth University
- Slade School of Fine Art
- York St John University.

The most important element of the application is the quality of the portfolio. There are three standard processes.

- Some universities ask you to submit your portfolio and/or examples of your work, usually online.
- You are invited to appear in person with your portfolio. Interviewers do not discuss the portfolio with you. You may have a tour of the school while it is assessed.
- You are invited to appear in person and you engage in a conversation with a tutor about the portfolio.

"We do this typically for design students so we can understand their capabilities in research, visual communication and skill base. A portfolio allows the student to describe their ideas and acts as a reminder to talk about present and past projects. It also reveals their personality, which is also fundamentally important when applying for a course to see how competently they can verbally communicate as well as being a team player and work with other students on the course."

ADMISSIONS, YORK ST JOHN UNIVERSITY

What follows is how two of the 10 institutions listed opposite select their candidates. While this will provide you with an insight into the process, remember these are examples from just two of many and you need to make an informed choice based on your own needs and research.

Kingston University, London

Kingston is a popular art Foundation course based near London. It interviews most applicants and the interview is based around the portfolio: a selection of work that the applicant has done, normally as part of the A level course, which best presents their interests and skills.

Interview format and outline

Kingston asks for all portfolios to be submitted online via Dropbox. The portfolio will consist of up to 40 photos of work and the applicant must specify the original dimensions of each piece. The photos must be well lit and taken with a good camera. Most sixth-form applicants can ask for support from their school in the preparation of these portfolios.

The photos must include examples of observational drawings using a range of different materials (pencil, pen, oils, watercolour, etc.). There should be photos of sketchbook work such as research, tests and idea development, photos of 'things that I like' and five finished pieces. **The portfolio is assessed and the best applicants are invited to an interview.**

There will be an informal group interview and a panel interview. You will discuss your work in both, and in the group interview you will be encouraged to comment critically and positively about other applicants' work. They are looking for a student who is open and willing to learn from others and takes an active interest in the world of art.

Arts University Bournemouth

This is another popular course that has a good reputation. It provides a similar range of teaching and assessment, with an emphasis on bridging the gap between A level and a degree course in art and design.

Interview format and outline

The interview will last about 20 minutes and will be a one-to-one interview with an academic. The focus will be on the portfolio of work you present, your interests and your career aspirations. The interviewer will talk about what influences your artwork, what artists inspire you and recent galleries you have visited that have influenced your thinking. They will ask about influences from other media too, including literature, cinema and advertising.

Again, the portfolio should be diverse and larger pieces should be photographed. Unlike at Kingston, the portfolio is assessed on the day. Bournemouth's advice about the portfolio is similar in places to Kingston's, but subtly different too.

- **'Drawing:** *A range of work including drawing from direct observation; drawing as problem-solving; and drawing to develop and present ideas.*
- **Idea/Design Development:** *Showing how you develop your ideas and designs. We would like to see sketchbooks and worksheets which show your development, experimentation with media and work in progress.*
- **Formal Elements:** *Work that demonstrates your understanding of the key principles of line, tone, perspective, colour, composition, form and space.*
- **Self-initiated Work:** *We would like to see examples of creative work which you have done outside of formal study.*
- **Contextual Understanding:** *Work that demonstrates your interests and understanding of arts, design and media practice such as illustrated essays, artist or design research and evidence of exhibitions you may have visited.'*

The portfolio should also show a range of media use. This could include painting, graphics, photography, film, ceramics, screen printing, model making, furniture and animation.

Interview tips

- Remind yourself of the course content and prepare some questions to ask at the interview about the course and the number of students who graduate and stay at the university to do a fine art degree. Look at the prospectus, and if possible visit the site before the interview to get a feel for the place.
- Take time to talk about your portfolio with a teacher at school or a trusted adult.

Think about what influences your work and how it has developed throughout the two-year A level course.

◗ Consider your post-graduation plans and have a good answer to the career aspiration question.

◗ Be prepared to talk in depth about an artist you cite in your personal statement.

◗ Think about films, books, posters, TV adverts or even the natural world. How do they influence you?

◗ Do you have a favourite genre of artwork?

◗ Think about the impact art has made on society and how you want your art to influence others.

◗ At interview, you may be asked to talk about a recent gallery visit, an architectural design that caught your eye or a news item about art. As one interviewee said to me: *'They will be seeking evidence that you are open to intellectual and artistic challenge, and that your work demonstrates that you have a curiosity towards creative experimentation and visual exploration.'*

RECOMMENDED READING

◗ Hern, Nick, *So You Want to Go to Drama School?* Nick Hern Books, 2010

◗ Vindbjerg, Ib, *The First Book I Wish I'd Had at Art College*, Ib Vindbjerg, 2017

TOP TIP

If you don't know how to answer a question, try brainstorming out loud!

© The University of Manchester

Physiotherapy

What is physiotherapy?

The definition from the **Chartered Society of Physiotherapists'** (CSP) of a physiotherapist is a *'professional who helps people affected by injury, illness or disability through movement and exercise, manual therapy, education and advice. They maintain health for people of all ages, helping patients to manage pain and prevent disease. It is a science-based profession and takes a "whole person" approach to health and well-being, which includes the patient's general lifestyle.'*

Background to the course

To become a physiotherapist, you will undertake a degree-based course (normally a three-year BSc) and this will combine lectures with on-the-job placements. Physiotherapists use their knowledge and skills to improve a range of conditions associated with different systems of the body, such as:

- **neurological:** stroke, multiple sclerosis, Parkinson's
- **neuromusculoskeletal:** back pain, whiplash-associated disorder, sports injuries, arthritis
- **cardiovascular:** chronic heart disease, rehabilitation after heart attack
- **respiratory:** asthma, chronic obstructive pulmonary disease, cystic fibrosis.

Physiotherapy is a vocational course leading to accreditation by the CSP. As such, all the courses will be similar with a mix of lectures, placements and work experience. You will meet patients early in the course and it is important at interview to show that you have the personal skills to cope with this patient-orientated career. Most courses are three years long but some are four, where there is a chance to take an integrated master's (MSc).

Learning within the clinical arena is an important and compulsory part of the course. All students have to successfully complete a minimum of 1,000 hours of practice education during the programme to be CSP accredited. Some placements are in hospitals and others in community settings. The course can have shorter holidays to accommodate these placements, and this does have a cost implication. You may also have to work at the weekends – it is important to remember that the NHS is a seven-days-a-week service and that by the time you graduate ALL NHS practitioners will be required to work some weekends.

Interview format and outline

Competition for places is high and universities will normally interview all applicants. This may be a one-to-one, panel or group interview, but more and more departments are using MMIs (see pages 68–70). The interview at **King's Colllege London** is arranged as follows:

- registration and pre-interview preparation (30 minutes)
- MMI (25 minutes)
- numeracy and literacy tests (40 minutes); sample tests are available online.
- tour of the campus (30 minutes).

....

"If your application is shortlisted, you will need to successfully complete a literacy test, numeracy test and a multiple mini interview (MMI) before you can be made an offer. It is expected that the selection event will last for around two-and-a-half hours, however; this is subject to change.

An MMI uses a series of booths or stations each with one interviewer in. Interviewers will ask questions to assess specific skills and qualities. You will have a set amount of time at each station, and when this is complete you will move on to the next station. This means that the same interviewer will ask the same question to all applicants. This allows us to assess candidates on a like for like basis."

KING'S COLLEGE LONDON

In addition, admissions tutors expect to see evidence of work experience to support your application. If successful, you will be subject to a Disclosure and Barring Service (DBS) check and healthcare screening to assess your suitability to work with vulnerable people. This is true of ALL physiotherapy applicants to any university.

....

"Candidates should be advised to make early applications to observe physiotherapists working in a variety of clinical settings to discuss their experience in the personal statement section of the UCAS form. Experience in a paid or voluntary capacity working with the general public, children, elderly or people with special needs will also help to strengthen an application."

ADMISSIONS, UNIVERSITY OF LIVERPOOL

Sample questions

Why do you want to be a physiotherapist?

This is one of the favourite questions that you can expect in any interview. The worst thing you can do is say that you have always wanted to be a physiotherapist; this doesn't give the interviewer much information. Instead, focus on the skills you possess to help you achieve your ambition. Talk about your work experience placements and what you learnt on them. Talk about your understanding of the place of physiotherapy in the NHS. Mention the words **cardiorespiratory**, **neurology** and **musculoskeletal** in your answer to counter the misconception that all physios do is treat sports injuries and work for football teams.

Cardiorespiratory patients need help with their heart and lungs and you will assist with their breathing, oxygen transfer or help a new patient who has cystic fibrosis. Neurology physios work with those with conditions which involve the nervous system, i.e. the brain, the spinal cord and the peripheral nerves (nerves away from the spine). This may involve helping people who have acquired brain injuries or those with multiple sclerosis. Finally, musculoskeletal refers to conditions that affect the muscle and skeletal systems, which can include most things people normally associate physios with, such as sports injuries, neck pain, back pain and post-operative pain.

NEVER say '**I want to be a physio so I can work for [e.g.] Arsenal**'. Wait until you have completed your first two years and then you can start to think about career plans.

How do you handle stress?

This is a common question and probably one of the most difficult questions you will get. The NHS is a high-pressure environment and admissions tutors will want to know whether you have the character to cope in such an environment. Don't make the mistake of claiming that you never get stressed because everyone does at some point. Instead, tell them about things that you have found stressful and why, and then talk about how you coped with the situation.

What qualities do you have and how will they enable you to be a good physiotherapist?

This is a common question and the advice I have been given is clear. Your answers need to include the phrases: **'I manage my time well and I keep good time'** and **'I would consider myself a compassionate person who is happy to listen to people and act on what I hear.'** Clearly, you may be asked to expand on these answers, so think about how you might do so. In addition, they want to hear that you have **good communication skills, are able to understand new information quickly** and that you are open to working with patients and staff **from all cultures, backgrounds, ages and beliefs.** This is important in the NHS, where you treat the patient first and foremost, regardless of who they are. Once again, be prepared to evidence these claims with examples of how you have shown these qualities at school, on a work placement or in another environment.

Other common questions

- Why did you apply to study at this university?
- What do you think is the most challenging aspect of a physiotherapist's job?
- Do you know what other types of professional people you'll be working with in the role?
- What are the advantages and disadvantages of home physiotherapy?
- Give us an example of when you had to overcome a difficult situation.
- What are the negative aspects of working in the NHS?
- Do you have any work experience related to physiotherapy? What did you enjoy about it and what did you learn?
- What is the role of the Chartered Society of Physiotherapy?
- Should we always treat a patient, even if they refuse treatment?
- How would you cope working with a patient with mental health or learning needs?

RECOMMENDED READING

- Barton, James, *Getting into Physiotherapy Courses*, Trotman Education, 2016
- Chartered Society of Physiotherapy: www.csp.org.uk

Social work

What is social work?

Social workers face complex and challenging situations and need to be committed to the principles of social justice. All social workers in the UK work in a stressful but rewarding environment, where 'soft' social skills are as important as academic ones. One leading practitioner I spoke to found it hard to define the role but used these words: *'It is a little like moulding clay. It is a process of giving shape and design to the messiness of human life. It takes psychological and scientific skills and knowledge but also more'*. She went on to describe a saying from her cultural heritage that summed up the key skills they look for in a good applicant: *'Our elderly fathers have got a beautiful saying "have an ear like an elephant in order to be able to listen to needs of others and have an eye like an eagle in order to see deep, the future and the present; have a heart like a lion in order to be positively bold and to give warmth to the cold feelings".'*

As a social worker, you will find yourself supporting people from a wide range of backgrounds. They may be children seeking help, parents struggling to cope with their children, school teachers with concerns about pupils, GPs who have concerns about patients, people with learning needs, physical disabilities or mental health issues, or just an elderly client who is lonely.

All those applying to read social work at university are routinely interviewed as part of the screening process. This interview will have several functions. It will ensure that you have the social skills that the interviewers are looking for. It will check that your motivation to study the course is founded on a sound understanding of the profession and, finally, that your academic profile meets the minimum requirements of the course.

Most UK university courses will have a similar structure. **Lancaster University**, which helped with the writing of this profile, offers two practice placements that form an important and integral part of this vocational degree. These are an excellent way of getting to know the role of a social worker and give you hands-on experience to back up your academic learning. This ensures that when you graduate you are prepared for work in the rapidly changing environments of social care.

....

"The two first-year modules, Social Work Practice and Contemporary Social Problems, will give you an introduction to the nature, origins and values of social work and to the economic, organisational policy and social circumstances in which it is practised. You will set issues in the context of class, gender, race and ethnicity, and disability to start developing a critical understanding of social work. Your first placement starts at the beginning of the September before your second year and runs through to mid-December. You then complete a series of modules that include Social Work with Children and Families, Social Work in Adult Social Care and The Research-minded Practitioner.

"Your third-year modules include Mental Distress and Health and, uniquely to Lancaster, Social Work and Drug Use. In addition, all social work students write a dissertation. Your final practice placement runs from January to May of your third year."

ADMISSIONS, LANCASTER UNIVERSITY

The skills that the selectors look for in a good applicant vary, but overall, they want to see that you have sound literacy, that you are a team player, have empathy and an awareness of the challenges of the profession and that you have some form of relevant work experience to support your application. This may or not may be with a social worker. They look for evidence that you have worked with children or vulnerable adults. For instance, experience at an after-school club, a local old people's home, a hospice or another similar venue where your social skills will have been enhanced.

"Experience in a paid or voluntary capacity working with the public, children, elderly or people with special needs will also help to strengthen an application."

ADMISSIONS, UNIVERSITY OF LIVERPOOL

Interview format and outline

Although each university has different processes, the common format is as follows.

- The candidate is invited to attend an interview. On arrival they are given an hour to read and consider a real case study. This will be referred to in the formal interview.
- The candidate may be asked to complete a paper questionnaire that assesses their motivation to study, knowledge of the laws relating to social care and how much the student knows about the course.
- There may be a **group discussion** – this will probably be to discuss a topical issue. They will be looking for you to shine, and it is likely that the discussion will be observed by an academic, a current social worker and a local GP. They will be

looking for you to show **good listening skills, empathy, emotional intelligence, positive body language** and **an inclusive manner**. This is a very important part of the process.

💬 There may be a final one-to-one interview that will be formal and in which interviewers will discuss your application and personal statement and see how you respond to some standard questions. This will last 20 minutes.

💬 All applicants will be required to undertake a Disclosure and Barring Service (DBS) check and standard medical clearances.

"Places on the BSc (Hons) Social Work degree are limited, so don't throw your chance away by being unprepared. This is your opportunity to sell yourself and show the panel what you can contribute to the profession. Answer the questions as fully as you can and give illustrations from your own life/career. Project warmth and confidence as you enter and don't forget to smile and make eye contact with the panel."

ADMISSIONS, UNIVERSITY OF SOUTH WALES

Sample questions

Why do you want to be a social worker?

It goes without saying that this is a key question and one that you need to have prepared for. Be honest about your own experience. Some social work applicants that I have known have drawn on first-hand experience of working with a social worker to promote their interest in the course. If you, or a member of your family, have worked with a social worker, then do not be afraid to allude to this. Keep confidentiality, though – this is an important function of any healthcare professional. If referring to real incidents, do not name the individuals as this would lead the interviewer to question your integrity.

Describe what you think a social worker does and what type of people or groups you might work with.

Again, this is a question that begs to be prepared for in advance. Make sure that you have read the information on the Community Care website (www.communitycare. co.uk). This is a portal for information about the profession and a must-read before your interview. Be prepared to talk about your work experience and what you learnt from it. Don't show a lack of awareness of the role of social work in the community, as this will indicate a lack of seriousness in your application.

Describe your understanding of the Code of Practice for Social Care Workers. How should it inform the daily work of social workers?

This question is common and refers directly to the agreed Code of Practice for Social Care Workers. This is a list of statements that describe the standards of professional conduct and practice required of social care workers as they go about their daily work. It goes without saying that you must have read this before the interview. It is available online at www.scie.org.uk.

NOTE: *Some universities (including the University of Wales) will ask you to complete a questionnaire that will ask about this code as part of the selection process.*

Other common questions

- What do you think are the qualities of a good social worker? How do your talents and skills match these?
- Describe a stressful or demanding role you've had and explain how you coped with it.
- Tell us about a time in which you contributed to effective team working.
- What current issues in the media regarding social work are you aware of?
- What is advocacy?
- What is the cycle of disadvantage?
- What is empowerment?
- What is discrimination, and can you provide an example of this?
- How do you manage your time?

RECOMMENDED READING

- Doel, Mark, *Social Work, The Basics*, Routledge, 2012
- Holland, Sally, *Social Work, A Very Short Introduction*, Oxford University Press, 2015

Veterinary medicine

What is veterinary medicine?

Studying veterinary medicine will allow you to gain a professionally recognised qualification, which will enable you to practise as a veterinary surgeon. Making the decision to become a veterinary surgeon will set you on a course for one of the most varied and exciting careers available. Only eight institutions offer veterinary medicine in the UK – Bristol, Cambridge, Edinburgh, Glasgow, Liverpool, London (Royal Veterinary College), Nottingham and Surrey. Competition for places is fierce, and entry requirements are high.

Notice for students applying to Cambridge

Remember to register for the BMAT, as it is a requirement for entry to the veterinary medicine course at this university. The University of Cambridge Local Examinations Syndicate (UCLES) states that: *'Students who don't take the BMAT won't receive an admissions interview.'*.

Background to the course

As a vet, you will need good communication skills – listening, writing and speaking – and motor skills such as good hand–eye coordination, dexterity and precision. All vet schools will expect that you have gained some animal-focused work experience, preferably in a range of animal-related areas such as at a veterinary practice, working with horses or on a farm, at a zoo or wildlife park, in research or laboratory settings or at an abattoir. You would be expected to understand the positive and negative aspects of a veterinary career and have an awareness of current important issues and developments in veterinary medicine.

It is important that you possess personal attitudes and attributes that are needed to be successful both on the course and in a veterinary career, including a caring ethos (compassion, tolerance, patience, empathy) and a sense of social responsibility. You should be able to cope with change and uncertainty and to overcome challenges while understanding your own limitations. Schools expect applicants to possess self-motivation, self-confidence, self-reliance and initiative. You should be able to show that you can work independently and as part of a team, and that you can integrate, cooperate and be flexible. Good personal organisational skills and time-management skills are a must.

Interview format and outline

Each university has its own process for selection and interviews. I have chosen to look at three schools but much of this information and that about other schools is available on the universities' web pages. It is important that you look at this carefully to ensure that you know, as best as you can, what to expect. This information will also be up to date.

University of Nottingham

Nottingham has a stated aim of encouraging a more diverse range of people to study the subject and places a very high value on widening participation. This is essentially an initiative to encourage applications from people who are under-represented at UK universities and applies to all universities and courses. Veterinary medicine is a subject that for many reasons receives few applications from ethnic minorities or from those whose personal circumstances have been challenging while at school and which have had an inevitable impact on their performance. (The Royal College also is keen to increase diversity in the profession to better represent the communities that vets work in and serve.) To that end, Nottingham uses an online survey as part of its initial screening. This is to ask information pertinent to widening participation and to ensure that the minimum six weeks' work experience criteria have been met.

"Information is requested to provide identification of any potential disadvantaging circumstances that may make progression to the veterinary medicine and surgery course difficult. This is also reviewed in the light of data provided by UCAS."
UNIVERSITY OF NOTTINGHAM

The school also uses what is known as a Situational Judgement Test. This is an online test, conducted before the interview, and is sat after the 15 October application deadline. It is 30 minutes long and can be taken only once.

The aim of the test is to assess whether the candidate has the *'key attributes that have been identified as important for veterinary students; they are concerned with testing interpersonal oriented skills and ethical values rather than knowledge or clinical skills.'*

Note this emphasis on interpersonal skills. Nottingham is looking for four key qualities, other than academic, in its young vets:

1. empathy
2. professional integrity
3. resilience
4. teamwork.

Before you take the test, make a checklist of your interpersonal skills and how you could demonstrate these four key attributes. This will help to focus your mind. Look too at some of the ethical questions that you may be asked at interview (see page 113) to help with the ethical integrity assessment.

The interview itself

Once you have been selected for interview, you can expect the following.

There will be a **panel interview** that lasts about 20 minutes. It will be conducted by two people, one of whom will be a practising vet. The interview will be formal but every attempt will be made to put the applicant at ease. The questions will vary, but will focus on *'academic ability, communication skills, animal-orientation, personal attitudes and attributes, fitness to practise as a veterinary surgeon'*. Be positive and shake hands with each of the interviewers. Smile, relax and listen carefully to the questions put. Take a moment to think about the answer, ask for clarification if you need.to and speak confidently and at a normal pace. Look the person who asked you the question in the eye when you answer, but look too at the reaction of the other interviewer.

There will then be a **Practical Aptitude Test**. This will last about 20 minutes and it will not assess an applicant's knowledge but it may involve animal handling, clinical information and some numerical questions. They are looking for *'enthusiasm and aptitude including observational and analytical skills and animal-orientation'*.

Finally, there will be a **Group Task**, which will be observed by the assessment panel. Here the selectors are looking at how well an applicant interacts with others and their body language. NOTE: show enthusiasm, but do not attempt to dominate the conversation.

University of Edinburgh

The Edinburgh Bachelor of Veterinary Medicine and Surgery (BVM&S) interview format is the MMI, and very similar to the model used for medicine (see pages 68–70).

Applicants will be asked to move between the separate stations; each station has a different assessor and each one lasts 10 minutes. There are seven stations:

- work experience
- career exploration and awareness of being a professional
- scientific data interpretation
- awareness of animal welfare
- moral and ethical dilemma
- practical manual task
- numeracy.

Five of the stations are staffed by an admissions tutor, who will ask questions or observe. Information from all seven stations will be used, together with the application form, to make a decision about whether to admit an applicant.

Royal Veterinary College (RVC)

"The RVC admissions process has recently changed and will now incorporate multiple mini interviews (MMIs). This involves working your way around a series of individual, timed stations designed to test specific competencies, such as communication skills, problem solving, numeracy skills and ethical awareness amongst others."

As with any veterinary college using MMIs, you will get some basic numeracy questions in the maths MMI, but these are straightforward and normally relate to calculating the proper dosage with certain facts in front of you. Just take a deep breath and think carefully!

Sample questions

It is important to stress that these are not the only questions you could be asked and you should do your own research. Look at the relevant university and professional websites, such as the British Veterinary Association's website (www.bva.co.uk), the RVC website (www.rvc.ac.uk), and even listen to the *Farming Today* podcast on Radio 4. These all have up-to-date information about rural and livestock issues. Some of the topics that might be worth thinking about include animal testing, bovine tuberculosis and the badger cull, pet obesity, antibiotic and antihelminthic (wormer) resistance, compulsory microchipping of dogs, avian flu, race horse management ... These are all issues that are in the news and which may be drawn out in an interview. Can you participate in debate on a subject that seems to have no right or wrong answer? Are you able to think on your feet when faced with difficult questions?

The following questions are designed to help you prepare for an interview. You should prepare some answers on paper first and then use them as the focal point for mock interviews. However, do not attempt to learn stock answers. Admissions tutors want to hear what you have to say and not what you think they want to hear. Do your research, be yourself, have the courage of your convictions and speak confidently about why you want to study the course.

Why do you want to be a vet?

This is clearly a key question that you need to think through in advance. It is an opportunity to promote your love of animals, their care and your own work experience, all of which will have helped you to make the decision to apply.

Why have your chosen this school?

This is another obvious question. Think about the nature of the course and what drew you to apply to this one and not others. Be careful to research the strengths of the course, the nature of the course and its teaching methods, and the practical placements offered.

What are your motivations?

This is a question that seems to want to draw out your motivations to be a vet. Are they honourable or realistic? Think in advance about your answer to this common question.

Royal Veterinary College sample questions

The RVC focuses on four key areas – your knowledge of science and ethics, communication skills, work experience and your expectations of a career in veterinary medicine.

Your knowledge of science

- When did you first realise you had an aptitude for the sciences?
- What subjects particularly interest you in science?
- What topics in biology or chemistry did you find most enjoyable and why?
- Talk us through a piece of coursework or an experiment that you completed and explain what you learnt.
- Do you read beyond the textbooks? If so, give us some examples.

In this section, interviewers are looking for evidence of curiosity – have you merely learnt a set of facts for the exams or have you really thought about the work you have been doing and asked questions/found out more?

Communication and non-academic interests and skills

- What do you consider to be your greatest strengths and weaknesses?
- How would you describe yourself?
- How do you deal with conflict situations?
- Tell us about your hobbies or interests beyond the classroom.
- Have you been a leader or taken the initiative in some way?
- Can you think on your feet?
- Give an example of how you overcame a problem that involved other people.
- What is the last book you read?
- Are you a morning or a night person?

Work experience

- Tell us about one of the work experience placements you refer to in your personal statement.
- Tell us about the work experience you have carried out since you applied.
- What did you learn about the different careers that you observed during work experience?
- What did you do on work experience? Were you given the chance to handle an animal?
- Were there any interesting cases/situations/events that prompted you to go away and look for further information?
- Can you talk about them in more detail?
- Would you see yourself working in a rural or town practice? Why?

Your expectations of the career

- Have you taken time to investigate and reflect on the key ethical issues and challenges facing vets, nurses and animal scientists today?
- What is the working day of a vet like?
- What is the role of a vet in the important area of public health?
- What is the difference between animal rights and animal welfare?
- Could you euthanise an animal?

RECOMMENDED READING

- Barton, James, *Getting into Veterinary School*, Trotman Education, 2017
- Royal College of Veterinary Surgeons: www.rcvs.org.uk – produces a free leaflet called 'Training to become a veterinary surgeon'.

Current developments in field of study

Whatever your chosen course it is important to keep as up to date as you can on developments in that field. For example, if you are applying for a healthcare related course you may wish to consider what new treatments are being developed?

Activity: Mind Map

We recommend that you use a mind map to brainstorm everything you know about the current developments in your chosen field of study.

Step 1: In the centre box write the subject area you are applying to.

Step 2: In the circles list:

- Any new research that is being done in this area.
- Any related news stories that are relevant to this field of study.
- Topics in your subject area that go beyond your course syllabus.
- What have you read in journals or on relevant websites?

It is important that you only talk about what you know.

If it's a subject like English or History for example, list some of the activities you have done to learn about this subject area outside of college, for example: read books that are not on the syllabus; visited museums etc.

Step 3: Use the lines off the circles to record your thoughts on these issues/developments.

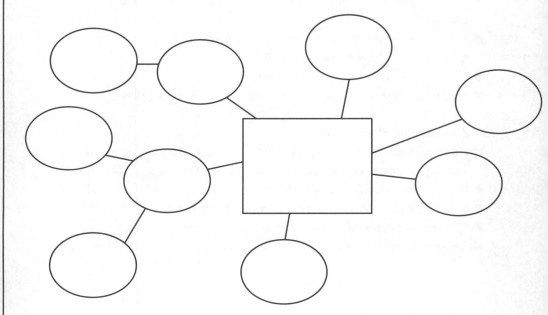

Extension activity: Can you answer the following questions?

- *Can you give me an example of a recent 'topical' development in this field of study that you may have seen in the media recently and do you have a view on this?*
- *What are you reading at the moment that is of interest?*

Oxbridge interviews

The Oxbridge (Oxford and Cambridge) interview is an event shrouded in myth and legend. However, the process is remarkably simple. Both universities receive a very large number of applications and they use the application form to carry out an initial screening – to eliminate the 'no hope' candidates from the rest. Most applicants who make the cut have predicted grades of three A grades at A level (most have better) and have a very good set of GCSE grades too. Clearly, if you are not taking A levels, then the equivalent grade is considered instead.

At Cambridge, around 75% of applicants can expect to be called to interview. This shows that applications to Cambridge are already quite self-selecting. At Oxford, the number called to interview is lower – between 40% and 80% – due to the number of entrance tests that are conducted before the final screening process. If you make the cut after this process, then you have a one in four chance of being made an offer. On average, one in five Cambridge applicants is offered a place.

The interviews normally take place in December, with results sent out in January. You are normally given two weeks' notice that you are being called to interview and many candidates arrive the day before and stay in accommodation provided free of charge by the college. Some colleges provide financial support to students for whom the travel costs would be prohibitive. This is means tested, so please ask. Widening participation is an important part of this process, so always make it clear to the university if you are from an ethnic minority, the first in your family to apply to university or come from a 'disadvantaged' background. Such contextual information is very important, so do let them know. If it is easier, send this information, with any supporting documentation (medical/social services etc.) by separate mail direct to the college you are applying to.

Most interviews take place in college and last between 20 and 30 minutes. The interview will be academic in focus and the candidate will be required to show critical thinking, creativity and a sound foundational knowledge of subject-specific content. This will not be the case where the subject is rarely studied at school. Here a general level of intelligence is ascertained, with questions that are designed to draw this out.

Interviewers are normally senior staff with plenty of experience of teaching and admissions. Sometimes the interview is conducted by the director of studies for the faculty in a college and often a second interviewer is present to take notes.

Oxford and Cambridge teach in a very special way. They do offer large lectures but much of the teaching takes place in college-based tutorials (at Oxford) or supervisions (at Cambridge). These are one to one or in small groups. They include direct feedback from the tutor and discussions that do not let anyone hide! To enjoy Oxbridge, you need to be someone who wants to work in this intense environment. Terms are shorter than at most other universities and the workload is high. Most colleges do not allow students to have paid work during term time and many offer grants to students from low-income families to allow them to avoid term-time work. The interview is designed to help the university find out whether you are the sort of person who will fit in. It is not for everyone!

The interviews are designed to closely model supervisions/tutorials. They are not aggressive and very rarely do they ask 'off the wall' questions – regardless of the myths about bananas and bricks. They are academically intense – but so is Oxbridge – so if that puts you off, don't apply.

The interviewers look not for knowledge of a subject (that is a given) but whether the candidate can adapt to new information and use current knowledge to bridge the gap between the two. They want to see critical analysis, excellent problem-solving skills, a love for the subject (where appropriate) and intellectual flexibility.

They do not look to take on pupils from certain schools, the sons or daughters of alumni, good rugby players or the affluent. That is old fashioned – it happened once, but is rarely the case now. Both universities actively seek those from state schools, and want to help students who lack the polish of the privately educated applicant. Oxford and Cambridge are arguably far more ordinary and egalitarian than many of the top, Russell Group universities, with their high numbers of independently educated, Oxbridge rejects!

The interviewers do want you to THINK OUT LOUD. As you think about the answer, speak about your thought process. Talk through how you are trying to solve the problem. Be prepared to ask them questions too. Never give up – be tenacious, show intellectual curiosity and be enthusiastic. Do say 'I need to take a moment to think about this' and maintain the conversation with questions or suggestions. The interviewer will help you out if you come unstuck – do not think that if this happens you are sunk. In fact, sometimes the opposite is the case. They want to see your POTENTIAL, not a finished product.

At Cambridge, all applicants will have one subject interview. Oxford often offers a general interview too. If appropriate, you may be asked to solve a problem, do some maths, translate something or read and then comment on an article. Always ensure that any work you sent in for assessment is re-read and that books you claim to have read have been read! The general interview will ask the usual opening questions – Why Cambridge? Why this course? Why this college?

Sample questions

How did you come to choose this course?

This is an opportunity to explain your motivation to read the subject, its origin in your academic process and what you have done, read or discussed to clarify this decision. There is no right or wrong answer to this question, so be true to yourself.

It is essential that you understand the nature of the course, what areas of the subjects are covered when, and what the college you have applied to specialises in. Look at the lecturers that are attached to the college and what their interests are. Know something about the history of the college.

Don't ever say that you are applying to please your parents or that your brother went there. This will cut no ice at all.

Do you think that you are clever?

This is a bit of a trap question. Clearly, most applicants ARE clever – academically anyway. So too are the interviewers! They want an answer that balances a realistic outlook with some humility. You might want to rephrase the question yourself by saying *'Well, I do think that I am academically intelligent, but would avoid the word clever as it has arrogant overtones. I am lucky that I am naturally inclined towards academic scholarship, but that does not mean that I am a better person than someone who is not. Indeed, some of the greatest entrepreneurs and leaders were not that academic, but they made it nonetheless. However, I am here to study (subject X) and at this stage, I am confident that I have the skills to do that well.'*

Why did you choose this college?

Again, this is a question that requires thought. You may have chosen the college for a variety of reasons, so be honest. It may be a large college (that suits you) or a smaller college (which also may suit). It may be one with a reputation in the subject or it could have a fine music tradition or chapel that attracts you. It could be that your family went to the college (tread carefully here). Whatever you say, avoid looking like you have not really thought this through in advance.

Other common questions

- Tell me about the impact Brexit may have on the UK economy.
- Tell me about something in the news that has grabbed your attention recently.
- Why should anyone go to university at all?
- What is your favourite novel?
- What is your favourite pastime?
- Who would you like to invite to have dinner with you, alive or dead?
- Can we trust our senses?
- Is maths true?
- Is an empty box actually empty?
- Are you the same person that you were before you walked into the room?
- Is there such thing as truth?
- Who has been the most influential person in your life and why?

Subject interviews

Unlike any other UK university, Oxford and Cambridge interview all shortlisted applicants to all subjects. Subject interviews are similar to general interviews, except that here the subject will be examined and discussed and matters relating to your UCAS form or outside interests will be ignored.

The format will vary, but overall the following is true.

1. You will be interviewed by one lecturer and another may be present to take notes.
2. The interviews will be in college rooms and quite informal in layout – expect sofas and armchairs, not desks and whiteboards!
3. The interviewers will be experts in their field and will ask you questions about the subject that are designed to stretch you. They do not expect you to know the answers, but they want to see how you cope with new information. They want to see you being creative, brave and willing to draw on other information to help you reach an answer.
4. You may be given some stimulus material – a bone, a plant, a piece of machinery, a banana! This is designed to spark a conversation. You may be given a puzzle to solve, a piece of translation to do or a document to read and comment on. Again – just take your time, think carefully and ask for help if you need it.

Don't be afraid to accept that you are wrong in a discussion. If you change your mind during a discussion, based on the nature of the discussion, it may well play in your favour. Intellectual arrogance is not actually something that humans like that much and Oxbridge dons (teachers) are humans! Show some humility where this is required.

Other advice when preparing

1 Ensure that you re-read any books that you claim to have read in the personal statement. Make sure too that you read another relevant book – there is a list of some good books recommended by tutors for different subjects on the following pages.

2 Watch a TED talk on the subject or be guided by a teacher about what to look for online. There are now many excellent lectures, given by top professors, that are online and free to view. NOTE: there is also a lot of rubbish out there, so always be guided by a teacher or adviser!

3 Practise interviews so that you can get used to proactively answering questions. Many schools offer mock interview practice. Try to find someone who you don't know that well, perhaps a family friend, who might interview you. Pick someone who is an experienced interviewer in a commercial environment or perhaps a graduate in the subject you aspire to study.

4 Sleep well the night before and arrive early for the interview. Lateness is discourteous and likely to cause stress levels to rise. Dress appropriately – clean, comfortable and conservative are my watch words.

5 SMILE and SHAKE HANDS. Maintain eye contact and thank people for seeing you.

6 Chat to other candidates but also remember that this is a 'game', so take their comments with a pinch of salt.

7 Find out a little about the college and, if possible, something about the interests of the dons at the college where you will be interviewed. To mention this in the interview will go down well – people like to be flattered.

8 Expect to be nervous – everyone is nervous, sometimes the interviewer is too. This is normal.

9 Don't rehearse scripted answers to questions – they will be obvious.

10 Do prepare answers to common questions and try your best to answer a question. Don't give up!

RECOMMENDED READING

Biology and medicine

- Dawkins, Richard, *The Selfish Gene*, Oxford University Press, 1976
- Gawande, Atul, *Being Mortal*, Profile Books Ltd, 2015
- Goldacre, Ben, *Bad Pharma*, Fourth Estate, 2012
- Pemberton, Max, *Trust Me I'm a (Junior) Doctor*, Max, Hodder & Stoughton, 2008
- Roach, Mary, *Stiff, The Curious Life of Human Cadavers*, Penguin, 2004

Chemistry

- Atkins, P.W. *Atkins' Molecules*, Cambridge University Press, 2003
- Sack, Oliver, *Uncle Tungsten: Memories of a Chemical Boyhood*, Picador, 2001
- Timbrell, John, *The Poison Paradox: Chemicals as Friends and Foes*, Oxford University Press, 2005

Economics

- Chang, Ha-Joon, *23 Things They Don't Tell You About Capitalism*, Penguin, 2011
- Levitt, Steven D. and Stephen J. Dubner, *Freakonomics*, Penguin, 2006
- Lewis, Michael, *The Big Short: Inside the Doomsday Machine*, Penguin, 2011
- Roubini, Nouriel, *Crisis Economics: A Crash Course in the Future of Finance*, Penguin, 2011

Engineering

- Forbes, Peter, *The Gecko's Foot: How Scientists are Taking a Leaf from Nature's Book*, Forth Estate, 2005
- Gordon, J.E, *Structures: or Why Things Don't Fall Down*, Penguin, 1991
- Petroski, Henry, *To Engineer is Human: The Role of Failure in Successful Design*, Vintage Books, 1992

Geography

- Carson, Rachel, *Silent Spring*, Penguin, 1963
- Marshall, Tim, *Prisoners of Geography: Ten Maps That Tell You Everything You Need To Know About Global Politics*, Elliot & Thompson, 2015
- Matthews, John A. and Herbert, David T. Matthews, *Geography: A Very Short Introduction*, Oxford University Press, 2008

History

- Carr, E.H., *What Is History?*, Penguin, 1990
- Marr, Andrew, *The History of Modern Britain*, Macmillan Publishers, 2007
- Tosh, John, *The Pursuit of History: Aims, Methods and New Directions in the Study of Modern History*, Longman, 1984

Human, social and political sciences

- Abercrombie, Nicholas, *Sociology: A Short Introduction*, Polity Press, 2004
- Schaffer, H. Rudolph, *Introducing Child Psychology*, Wiley-Blackwell, 2003
- Hay, Colin, *Why We Hate Politics*, Polity Press, 2007
- Hogg, Michael and Vaughan, Graham, *Social Psychology*, Pearson, 2013

Law

- Bingham, Tom, *The Rule of Law*, Penguin, 2011
- Kennedy, Helen, *Eve Was Framed: Women and British Justice*, Vintage, 1993
- McBride, Nicholas J., *Letters to a Law Student: A Guide to Studying Law*, Pearson, 2013
- Smith, A.T.H., *Glanville Williams: Learning the Law*, Sweet & Marshall, 2010

Philosophy, Politics and Economics (PPE)

- Heywood, Andrew, *Politics*, Palgrave, 1997
- Law, Stephen, *The Lives and Ideas of History's Greatest Thinkers*, Quercus Publishing, 2013
- Mill, John Stuart, *Utilitarianism*, Hackett Publishing Co, 2002
- Plato, *The Republic*, Penguin Classics, 2007

Physics

- DeGrasse Tyson, Neil, *Death by Black Hole and Other Cosmic Quandaries*, W.W. Norton & Co, 2014
- Kane, Kenneth S., *Modern Physics*, 3rd Edition, Wiley, 2012

Psychology

- Byron, Tanya, *The Skeleton Cupboard*, Pan Macmillan, 2015
- Pinker, Steven, *How the Mind Works*, Penguin, 1999
- Sacks, Oliver, *The Man Who Mistook His Wife for a Hat*, Picador, 2011

General good reading

- Agarwal, Rohan, *The Ultimate Oxbridge Interview Guide*, UniAdmissions, 2016
- Bates, Lucy, *Getting into Oxford & Cambridge 2018 Entry*, Trotman Education, 2017

PART THREE

HIGHER AND DEGREE APPRENTICESHIPS

CHAPTER SIX

THE HIGHER AND DEGREE APPRENTICESHIP ROUTE

For many years, the apprenticeship route was one favoured by those who preferred to work towards a trade, such as an electrician, plumber, builder or mechanic, rather than go on to higher education. However, the government recently relaunched the apprenticeship scheme and has rebooted the higher apprenticeship and introduced the degree apprenticeship route. If you are not sure that you want to study full time for a university degree, with all the costs that this entails, then this route may well be for you.

"I feel this route is suited to people who have come straight out of college but also to people like myself who have been in full-time employment and want to further their career by gaining some higher qualifications. It would be a big step to go straight back into full-time education, so I enjoy the balance of work life and student life."

SAM BUTLER, CHARTERED MANAGEMENT DEGREE APPRENTICE AT NOTTINGHAM TRENT UNIVERSITY

The new degree apprenticeship qualifications are pitched at 18-year-olds and offer a new way of combining work and the quest for a degree-level qualification. They are similar to higher apprenticeships, but differ in that they allow you to work towards a Level 6 (bachelor's) or Level 7 (master's) degree. You are employed by a company, even paid while training, and complete the degree qualification at a university that is working in partnership with the employer. The amount of time you spend at work and at university varies, but often you will work three days with the company and spend two days at university each week. You may also have to attend residential placements at certain points in the year.

Around 30 universities offer this new course, with others being added year on year. Indeed, the government recently announced a new fund worth £4.5 million to assist UK universities in setting up new degree apprenticeships. In April 2017, 5,200 more courses were offered; these new courses have been designed by employers and universities to ensure that the skills learnt are transferable.

"Apprenticeships work; that's why we've launched degree apprenticeships that give people a real chance to earn while you learn, putting you on the fast track to a top career. This multi-million-pound fund will allow universities and colleges to work with top employers to design high-quality degree apprenticeships that give people a ladder of opportunity, more choice and help shape Britain to become an apprentice nation."

SKILLS AND APPRENTICESHIPS MINISTER ROBERT HALFON (2016)

Degree apprenticeships are new, so there are only a limited number of vacancies available at the moment. UCAS suggests the following.

- Check out the range and number of vacancies being advertised in the area(s) you're interested in. This information is on the UCAS website. Check on a regular basis so you can get an idea of the availability of opportunities relevant to your interests.
- What is the timeframe from the vacancy being advertised to the application deadline and apprenticeship start date? This will give you an idea of how you need to prepare, and how quickly you will need to apply.

This is now a genuine alternative to full-time university study and you can work and train to gain the skills relevant to your employment in one of a range of jobs from engineering to retail management, and from accounting to law. The increasing number of different industry sectors now offering degree apprenticeships include:

- accountancy
- aerospace engineering
- aerospace software development
- automotive engineering
- banking relationship manager
- bespoke tailoring
- business and finance
- chartered surveying
- construction
- defence systems engineering
- electronic systems engineering
- IT/digital
- laboratory science

- law
- nuclear science
- outside broadcasting engineering
- power systems
- public relations.

UCAS offers-up to-date information online, with links to the courses that might be relevant to you. You can also look for information on the government website at www.findapprenticeship.service.gov.uk/apprenticeshipsearch.

Many major employers now offer these schemes – for a full list, look online, but a range are given here as examples.

Accenture

This company offers technology degree apprenticeships and places successful applicants in sites around the UK.

ARUP

The Arup apprenticeship gives you an unrivalled opportunity to put your skills to the test and your imagination to work on inspiring, high-profile projects.

"Our work within the built environment and infrastructure sectors across the country provides a fertile ground for us to recruit a number of apprentices in a number of areas – something which we will continue to actively support. Our approach will not only assist in providing us with the skills we need for the future, but also provide opportunities to those individuals interested in developing their careers in engineering, planning, design or business."

JOHN TURZYNSKI, DIRECTOR

Barclays Bank

The Bank offers a higher apprenticeship in collaboration with Anglia Ruskin University, called Business and Administrative Studies.

Barrett Development

This UK house builder has launched an innovative sponsored degree programme in construction, where all aspects of the construction process will be addressed both in the classroom and on site. This programme pays £24,000 while training, so is something to look at if this career appeals.

Bond Dickinson

This is a firm of solicitors, with offices throughout the UK, that is offering an apprenticeship programme that will enable those on the scheme to qualify as a solicitor without the need to study full time as an undergraduate.

Experian

Experian offers a sponsored degree in management and leadership at Nottingham Business School.

Flagship Group

This is a major UK company that provides homes for people in need. Its management degree is sponsored and, if successful, you will join the company as a graduate trainee.

Fujitsu

This global ICT company offers degree-level apprenticeships to applicants with three A levels. At the end of the four-year programme, you will have a degree and a foot in the door when applying for a graduate post.

KPMG

This major accountancy firm offers a six-year programme that gives you the opportunity to join the KPMG audit team, gain an accounting degree from either the University of Birmingham or Durham University and become a fully qualified chartered accountant. All your tuition and university accommodation fees are paid and you will receive a starting salary of around £20,000 (in London).

McDonalds

McDonalds offers a five-year sponsored degree programme, where you will end up with a degree in management. This can lead to a place on the McDonald Management Programme. This is a big step up from burger flipping!

Nestlé

The Nestlé Academy Fast Start School Leavers Programme allows you to study for a BA (Hons) degree in Professional Business Practice while gaining practical experience in a global business. You'll study at Sheffield Hallam University and combine this with placements in a number of business functions.

Santander

This Spanish clearing bank launched an apprenticeship programme in 2017 which involves working with a leading UK university to offer a cutting-edge banking and finance degree.

Unilever

This multinational company, which owns dozens of brands known to everyone, is offering a range of sponsored degree programmes, including research and development options. Once again, it will pay for the cost of the degree and you will have a good chance of getting a graduate job with the company once you complete the training.

The above are just few of the companies that offer support, and the number is increasing annually.

The universities that are involved at the time of going to print include the following.

- **Aerospace engineering and aerospace software development:** University of Central Lancashire and Lancaster University
- **Construction:** Anglia Ruskin University, Birmingham City University, University of Derby, Liverpool John Moores University, London South Bank University, Southampton Solent University and University of the West of England
- **Defence:** University of Bristol, Cranfield University and University College London
- **Digital industries:** Aston University, University of Exeter, University of Greenwich, Manchester Metropolitan University, University of Portsmouth, Queen Mary University of London, University of the West of England and University of Winchester
- **Life and industrial sciences:** University of Greenwich, University of Kent and Manchester Metropolitan University
- **Nuclear:** University of Bristol and The University of Manchester
- **Power engineering:** Coventry University
- **Surveying:** Birmingham City University, London South Bank University and University of Portsmouth.

For more information about these schemes and many others, look at the following websites:

- **UCAS – Degree apprenticeships:** www.ucas.com – search online for 'UCAS apprenticeships' for the latest information.
- **Prospects – Degree apprenticeships:** www.prospects.ac.uk – this is a useful site managed by Prospects, which has a list of degree programmes on offer and lots of useful information about how to apply and where to look. It is updated weekly, so it is far more up to date than this book could ever hope to be.

Should I consider this option?

The answer is yes, if you would prefer for financial or other reasons to work and study simultaneously. However, this is not an easy option for a variety of reasons.

- It is very competitive – entry to these schemes is prestigious, so you will need to ensure that you prepare well when you put together your application and if you are invited to an interview or assessment centre.
- You will possibly study for just one full day a week – this means that lots of work will need to be done in the evenings or at weekends to keep up. This will not suit the work-shy!
- You will need to be determined to cope with the workload and the pressure. However, if you do well it will help you to secure a role in a major corporate company and you will do so with little financial cost to yourself or your parents.

When you apply, you will need to show that you have some of the key 'soft skills' that employers look for in applicants with the potential to become managers.

Sponsors of degree apprenticeship programmes want to see evidence that you *enjoy working as part of a team*, that you are *not afraid to lead*, that you *enjoy independent learning*, that you are *self-motivated* and that you have *good communication* and *analytical skills*. Clearly, different employers and universities will have different academic expectations, but they will all be looking for similar personality traits.

If you are admitted on to a scheme the tuition fees will be paid by the employer or the government – this will amount up to a colossal £9,250 saving per annum. As you are being paid too, you can often live quite well without falling into debt. You may need to live away from home, so factor this into your planning so that accommodation issues do not bear too heavily on your choice of company and university. The graduate employment rate is also very high – in 2015 83% of those who completed the apprenticeship programme continued to work for the sponsoring company and most were promoted within 12 months.

Applications can be processed either via UCAS or via the UK government's Find an Apprenticeship website, www.gov.uk/apply-apprenticeship.

TIME TO BRAINSTORM: PREPARING FOR THE APPRENTICESHIP INTERVIEW

If the above interests you, then take a moment to find some paper and start to do some research.

Here is what to do now.

- Much of the information in Parts One and Two applies to you too. Read Part One carefully for some insight into the psychology and likely format of an interview.
- Chapter Four has a section on how to answer common interview questions. Again, I suggest you read this carefully too.

Other than that, here are some specific tips from well-known employers.

1 Well done if you are called for interview. Most applicants fail at the first stage, so make sure your application is excellent and free from errors or poorly evidenced claims about yourself. Do your research well in advance of completing the application.

2 Wear something comfortable, clean and, as this is a work interview, make sure you wear a jacket and tie, if male, or a smart dress or shirt/blouse with skirt/trousers if female. Keep it quite modest and business like. First impressions count!

3 Smile and shake hands when you meet the interviewer for the first time. Wait to be asked to sit down.

4 Know what the job or course requires. This is basic preparation. Understand the nature of the company, know some of its recent history, its products and competitors in the same industry. Read the annual report and accounts that are published online. Look to see if the company has been in the news recently or whether it has launched a new product.

5 Brainstorm some possible questions that you are likely to be asked. These would probably include those found in Section Two. Here are some other possible questions.

- How would your family or friends describe you?
- How would your school describe you?
- Why did you choose this industry?
- What do you know about our company and this scheme?
- What would you say are your primary strengths?
- How do you cope with stress?
- What projects have you led recently at school or college?

- Are you a leader or a follower? Give me an example.
- Why do you want to do this route rather than go straight to university?
- Do your parents support you in this application?
- Give an example of how you have dealt with a difficult situation.
- What do you think we mean by customer-focused service and how will it relate to this job?
- What is your understanding of equal opportunities and how they apply to this job?
- What is your attitude to work-life balance? Do you think you can cope with the pressure of working in the evenings or weekends to keep up with the degree course?
- Why should we appoint you and not the next applicant?
6   Make good eye contact, thank the interviewers for meeting you and show some enthusiasm.

TOP TIP

Practise speaking clearly and concisely; practise talking about yourself in a professional manner.

© The University of Manchester

Some final points to consider

As an apprentice you will enjoy the same legal rights as any other employee. You will receive a wage, sick pay, paid leave and access to all the normal health and safety legislation to protect you when at work. You will have a contract of employment, often called an Apprenticeship Contract, and you will also have a contract with the university or college offering you access to training. You will also be protected by the same anti-discrimination legislation as all other workers, which means that you cannot be treated any differently regardless of your age, gender, sexual orientation, race or religion.

A good website with information on all apprenticeships in the UK is The Apprenticeship Guide, www.apprenticeshipguide.co.uk, where information is updated weekly and is free to access. I am grateful for its support in putting this part of the book together. It offers impartial advice to applicants considering all types of apprenticeships, from post-GCSE applicants to degree apprentice applicants.

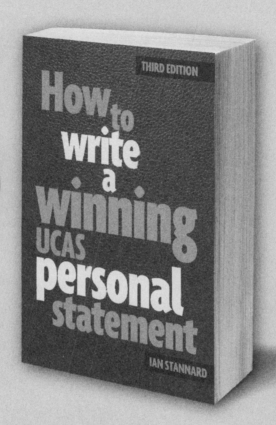